The Place Setting

Timeless Tastes of the Mountain South,
from Bright Hope to Frog Level

Second Serving

Fred W. Sauceman

Mercer University Press | 2007

MERCER
UNIVERSITY PRESS

Endowed by
TOM WATSON BROWN
and
THE WATSON-BROWN FOUNDATION, INC.

MUP H718

© 2007 Mercer University Press
1400 Coleman Avenue
Macon, Georgia 31207
www.mupress.org

Book design: Burt & Burt Studio

∞The paper used in this publication meets the minimum
requirements of American National Standard for Information
Sciences—Permanence of Paper for Printed Library Materials,
ANSI Z39.48-1992.

Library of Congress CIP

Sauceman, Fred William.
The place setting: timeless tastes of the mountain south,
from bright hope to frog level: second serving
p. cm. Includes index. Hardback.
ISBN-10: 0-86554-998-2   ISBN-13: 978-0-86554-998-2

1. Cookery, American. 2. Cookery–Appalachian Region, Southern.
3. Appalachian Region, Southern–Social life and customs.
I. Title.
TX715.S145248 2006   641.59756'8–dc22
2006004513

Contents

Waterfront Fare

Fancy Digs

From the Sugar Sack

Loaf and Linger

Recipes

We shall not cease from exploration
And the end of all our exploring
Will be to arrive where we started
And know the place for the first time.

T. S. Eliot, *Four Quartets*

Acknowledgments

I wish to thank my parents, Wanda Royall Sauceman and the late Fred Sauceman, Sr., for always making sure I was fed well. They boiled Silver Queen corn for me near midnight, canned kraut with the signs and saved me the cabbage stalk, slapped T-bones into hot iron skillets on Saturday nights, and took me out for chuckwagon steak at every roadside restaurant around.

I thank my wife, Jill, for her mountain sense and sensibilities, for gamely accompanying me to obscure and out-of-the-way places in search of food and stories, and for having the foresight, as a little girl, to absorb her grandmother's dried apple stack cake technique.

Our Yorkiepoo, Lucy, has proven to be a reliable recipe tester and has somehow managed to maintain her weight at 5 pounds, 8 ounces.

I thank Pamela Ripley, executive director of University Relations at East Tennessee State University, for reading every word I've written about food and for making insightful improvements in my stories.

Larry Smith, East Tennessee State University's talented, longtime photographer, has contributed many of the pictures that accompany these essays, and I deeply appreciate his work in documenting the foodways of our native Southern Appalachia.

Dr. Paul E. Stanton, Jr., popular and high-achieving president of ETSU, saw, early on, the value of our work in preserving and perpetuating mountain food culture and its relationship to the mission of our regional university. He has encouraged and inspired us constantly.

I am indebted, as well, to a kitchen full of other colleagues at ETSU: Jim Sledge, Janice Randolph, Linda Malone, Diane Nave, Kristn Fry, Joe Smith, Jennifer Hill, Carol Fox, Susie McLeod, Jeanette Henry, Rebecca Tolley-Stokes, and Amanda Barnhill Terry among them.

Wayne Winkler, manager of public radio station WETS-FM, Judy Harwood, and the staff there have helped produce our food-centered stories, spreading the gospel of beans and cornbread on the air and over the Web. I thank Giles Snyder, now with National Public Radio, and Beth Vorhees of West Virginia Public Broadcasting for airing our essays and stories on the weekly program "Inside Appalachia."

Keith Wilson, Ted Como, and Brad Lifford with the *Kingsport Times-News* deserve much credit for the creation of this book. They have given me an unregulated, weekly hunk of space so I can write about cushaw butter, Monster Ham sandwiches, and slugburgers. Thanks to David Grace of the *Times-News* for graciously allowing us to use his fine photographs.

Helena Jones and Kathy Knight from my hometown paper, the *Greeneville Sun*, have willingly shared column inches for my ramblings and ruminations about food.

Nicole Sikora began my rewarding relationship with *Marquee* magazine, and I am grateful to the current editor, Mary Ellen Miller, and to publisher Cathryn Russum for steering me to cinnamon rolls in Abingdon, Virginia, wild boar in Blowing Rock, North Carolina, and quiche in Kingsport, Tennessee. I appreciate Murray Lee for contributing two of his magazine photographs for this book.

I thank John T. Edge, Mary Beth Lasseter, Ann Abadie, Amy Evans, Ronni Lundy, John Egerton, and the members of the Southern Foodways Alliance, headquartered at the University of Mississippi's Center for the Study of Southern Culture, for their symposia, field trips, and friendships that have brought me to realize, anew, the value of the food traditions of my homeland. In particular, I appreciate Peggy Galis of Athens, Georgia, whose suggestion that we "get up and walk around" during the 2004 Southern Historical Association meeting in Memphis, led to the eventual publication of *The Place Setting: Timeless Tastes of The Mountain South, from Bright Hope to Frog Level*—volumes 1 and 2.

Bob Creswell of Kingston, Tennessee, reacquainted me with Roane County and reminded me about the denizens of the Roadside Café, including Butterhead Stout, the only plumber we've ever known with an unlisted telephone number.

Even though he added extra pounds and stuffed me into a gold jacket that isn't my color, I thank my friend Charlie Daniel, cartoonist for the *Knoxville News-Sentinel*, for plopping me down on a stool in his fictional diner, Rosy's, and drawing me a Rosyburger.

Ardie Davis with the Kansas City Barbeque Society kept us supplied in sauce. Allan Benton, pork prince of Madisonville, Tennessee, stocked us with country ham, smoked bacon, sausage, and prosciutto.

I thank the members of the news media in Northeast Tennessee and Southwest Virginia who have generously provided outlets for our slow food crusade—especially Lisa Kereluk-Whaley, who covered our very first food talk back in 1990, and Louise Durman, retired food editor for the *Knoxville News-Sentinel*.

Members of the Institute for Continued Learning at ETSU have patiently listened to our discussions on barbecue, catfish, blues, beans, and juke joints, and for that I owe them my gratitude.

I am also thankful for the confidence and encouragement of Director Marc Jolley, Marsha Luttrell, Kevin Manus, and Regenia Toole at Mercer University Press and for their desire to share these stories with a wider audience of readers.

Finally, and vitally, I thank the home cooks, restaurant owners, chefs, farmers, and artisanal producers who have opened up their kitchens, pantries, fields, barns, and hearts to us. May they find in these pages the recognition and honor their labors deserve.

The Cherokee poet and storyteller Marilou Awiakta once spoke to me of Spam. Marilou can always find profound meaning in the simplest and most unassuming of foods. She told me how, in the days of rationing during World War II, her family looked forward to a meal of the processed meat from a can. Her mother would score the top of a loaf of Spam, just like folks prepared hams in better times, mix a vinegar and brown sugar sauce to pour over it, and if she could find them, she'd decorate the top with red cherries.

"What I think is very Appalachian about that," Marilou said, "is making do with what you have, and do your best with it and don't whine. We had Spam and it was good."

That theme recurs in the words of the mountain people I've interviewed for the essays that comprise these two volumes. It's their kind of wisdom the world needs most desperately now, their ability to appreciate and to glorify the honest and the unadorned in an increasingly complicated world.

In this age of instant gratification, I have attempted to document the stories of people whose persistence has kept farms, restaurants, bakeries, and businesses going for half a century or more, despite all the pressures to conform to shortcut cookery or sell out to the megastores.

Imagine keeping a fried pie company afloat amid twenty-first-century food fears. Consider the challenges of overseeing a mill that opened during George Washington's presidency. Contemplate promoting a product called Pure Sugar Stick Candy in the era of *Sugar Busters*. Think about the struggles of selling regional, family-produced soft drinks strong in caffeine. Ponder promoting 14 percent butterfat ice cream.

These books celebrate generations of people who have had the courage to go their own way, to cling to proven, sometimes even ancient, techniques, to remain loyal to age-old flavors despite the existence of easier, less laborious methods. Those tastes and talents have come from as close to me as Roan Mountain in Northeast Tennessee and as far away as The Philippines.

It is my hope that, through food, these volumes tell a story of Southern Appalachian perseverance in an impatient era. I invite readers to visit these places, to inhale the scents of mills well over 200 years old, to buy brown bags of greasy beans picked right out of the field in July and cook them all afternoon with a pork hock, to picnic on mountain creekbanks. Step into these settings with cell phones off and pagers cast aside, and hear voices simple and lasting and strong.

Pioneers and Practitioners

We worship church-supper salad,
integrate with apple pie,
skirmish over peanuts and popcorn,
and buy burpsies.

Cussing Custard Pie

Three Early East Tennessee Television Cooks

In the fall of 2003 two East Tennessee television stations celebrated fifty years on the air. Both of them featured live cooking shows long before the advent of the Food Network, even before Julia Child started her *French Chef* series on the Public Broadcasting System.

At a time when locally produced television programs were aired live, Patty Smithdeal Fulton of Johnson City's WJHL and Mary Starr of Knoxville's WATE brought their sense of adventure, bright personalities, and culinary acumen into the region's homes. Patty and Mary were central figures in fiftieth-anniversary specials on the two stations. Patty lives in Johnson City. Mary, whose real last name was Walker, died in 1995.

Patty Smithdeal Fulton

"I was the production manager of WJHL at the time," Patty recounted in an interview with Kingsport's Sherilyn Twork, a student in my ETSU course "Foodways of the American South."

"We didn't know what we were doing. We were pioneers. The cooking show was originally done by another woman who really was more of a stage presence than a cook. She became ill one morning, and as I was the only woman on the staff at the time, I had to fill in.

"I don't remember what I cooked that first day. I think I made an asparagus casserole and rice ring. I tore downtown and got all the ingredients and rushed back and got ready. It was maddening, but I did it."

Having been born in her grandmother's boarding house in Elizabethton, Patty always had a mountain dweller's appreciation for a good custard pie.

As Sherry Twork related in her class essay "What's Cooking in a One-Woman Kitchen?" the set at WJHL was simple at the time, having just two cameras.

"It wasn't luxurious like TV studios today," Patty told Sherry. "At the end of the custard pie program, I showed the finished product, and when I

Patty Smithdeal Fulton. *Photo by Sherilyn Twork.*

pulled the pie out, I noticed the bottom was still warm. I cut it anyway, and as I couldn't find the spatula, I lifted it out with a knife and it just fell apart. Of course, the camera was on close-up. I later found out the fellows in the control room were saying, 'Cut the mike! Cut the mike! She might start cussing!' But I didn't."

Patty Smithdeal Fulton's Butter Pecan Bread

1 box butter pecan cake mix
4 eggs
1 small box coconut-flavored instant pudding
1 scant cup canola oil
1 cup very warm water
1 cup chopped nuts, such as pecans

Combine all ingredients except nuts. Beat well. Stir in nuts. Pour into two greased and floured loaf pans. Bake at 325 degrees for forty-five minutes or until a toothpick comes out clean.

Mary Starr

Among the many advantages of growing up in Greeneville, Tennessee, was my exposure to television stations in both the Tri-Cities and Knoxville markets. My grandmother Ethel Royall was a devoted fan of Patty Smithdeal Fulton to the northeast, Mary Starr to the southwest.

In 1965 Grandmother Royall suffered a severe stroke while bathing and the scalding water badly burned her feet and legs. For weeks she lay in the hospital near death. The doctor told us she would never take another step. Then one day, while lifting her out of bed, the hospital staff almost dropped her head-first toward the floor.

From that time on she began to improve and communicate, and after skin grafts and physical therapy she painfully learned to walk again. She moved to Athens to live with my aunt and uncle, Grover and Mary Nelle Graves. One day, when my aunt came home for lunch from her job in the president's office at Tennessee Wesleyan College, my grandmother ordered

Mary Starr. *Photo courtesy WATE-TV, Channel 6, Knoxville, Tennessee.*

her to get a pencil and pad. Giving orders was an additional sign that my grandmother was recuperating. She directed my aunt to write down a potato soup recipe she had memorized earlier that morning from Mary Starr's WATE channel 6 *Homemakers' Show.* Now, thirty-five years after my grandmother's death, we still prepare this potato soup as a way of remembering her triumph.

In 1970 Mary Starr published many of her popular television recipes in a cookbook, which was a complete sellout. In honor of the station's fiftieth birthday, the book was reissued as *Starr Recipes from Greystone*. The 3,000 copies of the reprint sold out in two months.

Mary Starr's Hearty Potato Soup

Peel and dice one medium potato for each serving. Chop a proportionate amount of onion and celery. Cover with water. Salt to taste. Cook covered until vegetables are tender. Stir in one teaspoon of cornmeal for each potato and cook about ten minutes longer. Fry until crisp two slices of breakfast bacon for each serving, then drain the bacon on a paper towel. Break the bacon into small pieces and add to cooked vegetables along with one cup of milk for each serving. Heat to serving temperature. Taste and correct seasoning.

Ilo Salyer

Piecing together a portrait of Ilo Birchfield Salyer is like working a jigsaw puzzle with edges frayed and rounded. My mind's image of her is as cloudy as the 17-inch picture produced by the Magnavox American Modern console television set, the focal point of our living room in the late 1950s and early 1960s. The set had a turntable in the top, an AM-FM radio below, and that ever-present brown grill cloth so familiar to bedroom disc jockeys like me.

My mental picture of Kathryn Willis, Ilo's successor at WJHL-TV, is clearer. By the time she came along the Magnavox plant in Greeneville, where my father worked, had begun turning out color television sets. We weren't the first in the neighborhood to buy one, but we weren't far behind Chester and Margaret Brent after we went over for a visit and saw what *The Wonderful World of Disney* looked like in color.

Kathy Gregory (now Hatjioannou), age five, models a dress during "Memo from Ilo," 1965. *Photo courtesy Al Gregory.*

Ilo, though, is black and white to me, and my attempt to fill in the color has been tough. She's nonexistent on the Internet and fading in the memories of other mid-twentieth-century television viewers. Most of her half-hour variety shows were live, unrecorded and lost forever.

I had been thinking about crafting a column on Ilo for several months, but no leads came my way. In December of 2004, we were eating in a restaurant in Wise, Virginia, when a lady named Iloe Stallard, a retired school administrator, introduced herself. I picked up on the uncommon first name immediately and inquired. She had been named for the early television personality, with an extra "e." She told me that Ilo's son Russell sold cars in Kingsport, Tennessee, and I tracked him down.

"There wasn't anything she couldn't do," Russell told me. "She raised tobacco and knew how to grade it. She poured concrete. She provided a trailer for me to take horses to shows. She knew how to cut ham and make sausage. She made blackberry wine in a 20-gallon crock, although I never saw her drink it. She was always reading, always seeking more knowledge. The words 'I can't' were not in her vocabulary. She was a brilliant woman."

Throughout the Tri-Cities Ilo taught adult education classes in ceramics and instructed students on the fine points of making ladies' hats. She raised pheasants on her 34-acre farm at Cole Springs, between Kingsport and Bristol, and used the feathers in her hat-making. She gave hats to Russell's teachers at Christmastime.

Born in Big Stone Gap, Virginia, Ilo was best known for her whistling, and she made the circuit among East Tennessee churches imitating birds, accompanied by the piano.

"There wasn't a bird she couldn't mimic," recalls Russell. "Her special call, her signal, for my sister and me to come in from playing was the whistle of the whippoorwill."

Memo from Ilo ran on WJHL from 1957 to 1966, thirty minutes a day, five days a week. Retired program director Al Gregory remembers the day Ilo brought live horses into the studio to promote a horse show.

"Cooking was probably the last of what she did," says Al. "She conducted fashion shows, demonstrated sewing techniques, and interviewed all sorts of personalities. She was a lovely person, easygoing, pleasant, and she met people well."

When she did cook, Russell says casseroles were her specialty, and she was one of the first to promote the concept of the one-dish meal.

"She made heavy chicken casseroles with fresh mushrooms she had picked," Russell remembers. "She talked about different ways to bake meat. And one of her favorite dishes to make on the show was a brandy fruitcake with real brandy."

When Kathryn Willis took over the program she had to keep the cooking segment, but former WJHL general manager Hanes Lancaster says kitchen expertise wasn't her strong point.

"She had gone to acting school in Palo Alto, California, and she also had radio experience during World War II, talking to the troops through Armed Forces Radio. She had a wonderful gift of gab. Whether she could cook or not, she'd pre-do it and then show it. She'd spend the morning before the show cooking, and everybody in the station would have lunch there off of what she cooked.

"Or else it'd go in the garbage can. She had interesting guests, though, and she handled it beautifully."

"Now Ilo, she could cook," says Hanes. "But she was so meticulous it would stretch out all day."

Ilo Salyer died in 1987.

Ilo's Salad

Cynthia Taylor Livesay of Kingsport, Tennessee, remembers her mother, the late Ruth Ketron Taylor, sitting in front of the television during *Memo from Ilo* with a notepad and pen ready to copy recipes. This one is from Ruth's files. It's classic 1950s covered-dish church fellowship hall fare.

1 cup coconut	1/2 cup celery, diced (optional)
1 cup fruit cocktail, drained	1 cup miniature marshmallows
1 cup cottage cheese, dry	1/2 cup chopped pecans
1 cup pineapple, crushed and drained	1 cup sour cream

Mix and place in the refrigerator. Let set for several hours then serve.

Trula Bailey's Stuffed Eggplant on the Half-Shell

This recipe has 1960s written all over it, from the reliance on Ritz crackers to the silver knife used to check for doneness. The original source is a booklet called *Ford Times,* once published by the motor company (my Uncle Grover Graves only drove Fords). I inherited the recipe from a lady named Trula Bailey, who for over fifty years worked in the home of my aunt and uncle in Athens, Tennessee. She was largely responsible for my grandmother's remarkable recovery and even had her crocheting again. Eggplant was exotic and mysterious to me as a child growing up in the 1960s, and the deep-purple color still entices me. Trula was the first person ever to serve it to me, and she gave me my first mushroom, too. She died in the winter of 2002, but her visage presides, in watercolor, over my dining room as her outstretched hand offers guests one of her incomparable, irresistible, and irreproducible whole-wheat muffins.

1 large eggplant, split lengthwise
Salt and pepper to taste
1 cup celery, chopped
1/4 cup onion, chopped
3 ounces butter
2 eggs, well beaten
1 cup milk
1/2 cup grated sharp cheddar cheese
1 cup Ritz crackers, rolled, plus extra for topping

Scoop insides from eggplant and cook in salt water until tender. Drain, chop, and season with salt and pepper. Cook celery and onion in butter until tender. Add with remaining ingredients to mixture. Return mixture to shells and place in baking dish. Sprinkle top with additional cracker crumbs. Bake one hour in a 350-degree oven, or until a silver knife inserted comes out clean. Serves four.

Clearing the Way
with Biscuits and Kindness

Chef Hyder Bundy
and the Quiet Integration of a Campus

I wish I had a recipe to accompany this essay. I wish I had met the person who is its subject. I never tasted Hyder Bundy's fried chicken or apple pie. I never profited from a kitchen-table conversation.

I only know Hyder Bundy through the memories of others whose souls and stomachs were fed by this quiet hero of the kitchen, now all but forgotten on the campus he nourished for over forty years.

From the one black-and-white photograph I have of him, I can tell he had the build of a chef, probably somewhere on the scale of corpulence between James Beard and Mario Batali. His white chef's toque is pushed back playfully on his head and tilted slightly to his left. I'd wager that Hyder Bundy loved his own cooking as much as the students, faculty, and staff of East Tennessee State College did.

His smile is real and kind and his hands lay loosely clasped in his lap. I would have liked Hyder Bundy.

He didn't sit behind a desk or around a boardroom table. He labored in the heat and obscurity of a small college dining hall. He and his family lived in the basement of East Tennessee State's first women's dormitory, Carter Hall. In the segregated Jim Crow South he couldn't take his family downtown to eat restaurant food or even bus-station grub.

He had come south in 1915 from Castlewood, Virginia, just four years after the opening of East Tennessee State Normal School, in search of a cooking job. What he undertook when he got there was a mission to spread kindness and compassion everywhere he went.

It's disturbing that there's so little written information on Chef Bundy in the expected places on the campus. There's hardly a trace of his presence in the university archives.

Chef Hyder Bundy. *Photo courtesy East Tennessee State University.*

Knowing what I do about his personality and the confidence President Burgin Dossett had in him, I credit Chef Hyder Bundy in large part for the peaceful and successful integration of the campus in January of 1956. The integration occurred almost two years after the United States Supreme Court's 1954 Brown v. Board of Education decision, which ordered the desegregation of the nation's public schools, and several years before integration occurred at other universities in the South.

At East Tennessee State there were no politicians standing in doorways, no Molotov cocktails, no threats and name-calling. Instead, Eugene Caruthers calmly walked through the registration line unbothered and entered graduate school before going on to direct the band at Langston, Johnson City's all-black high school that operated from 1893 to 1965. Hyder Bundy cleared the way for Eugene Caruthers and all the African-

American students who followed him—and he did so not by force but through the strength of a smile and a warm meal.

If Mr. Bundy were around today, he'd deserve a title like vice president for governmental relations. President Dossett depended on him heavily for political advice in the 1940s and 1950s. From the campus kitchen Chef Bundy gave Mr. Dossett guidance on Democratic politics and relationships with the local black community.

Religion writer Phyllis Tickle is the daughter of the late P. W. Alexander, who was once head of the Training School and later dean of the college. She remembered Chef Bundy this way:

"He was perfect for and with kids, having a bunch of them himself and a positive bevy of grandchildren who hung around—he called it 'helping me run the place'—the cafeteria on Sundays. His jovial kindness and his incredible biscuits were formative parts of my childhood as a campus brat. His fried chicken was the best in the South by his own admission, and his mashed potatoes were the best you'll ever eat here or in Heaven. What a great, gentle, regal old man he was."

Jean Copeland, who worked in the college's business office, remembers "people standing in line for Bundy's apple pies." Two years before he retired, the students dedicated the 1955 annual to him, "Our relentless, loyal and faithful cafeteria chef."

In his history of ETSU, Dr. Frank Williams tells of an alumnus complaining in 1954 that Chef Bundy no longer summoned students to meals by beating the iron triangle. The graduate claimed the sound stimulated his appetite and contributed to his appreciation of music.

Hyder Bundy never made the headlines, but he influenced thousands of students and coworkers, teaching them, through his unassuming grace and goodness and biscuits, the meaning of equality.

Pitching Chickens with Cas

Southern Appalachia's Most Colorful Grocer

The neon scissors don't snip anymore, but every once in a while, still today, after a good transaction you can hear a merchant tell a customer, "You can't beat that at Cas Walker's."

Born in 1902 in Sevier County, Tennessee, Caswell Orton Walker was Southern Appalachia's most colorful and controversial grocer. He worked as a young man in the Kentucky coal mines and saved $850. He used that money to buy a grocery store in Knoxville, Tennessee, and by the end of his long and contentious career, he lorded over a multimillion-dollar chain.

Outside each of his twenty-seven stores in Tennessee, Virginia, and Kentucky stood the constantly clipping "sign of the shears," one of several advertising techniques he developed himself with almost no formal education and certainly no training in sales and promotion.

One of Walker's favorite stratagems was to throw live chickens off the roof of a store. Customers who caught them could keep them. Women wore aprons to those events to haul in the birds.

Radio and television advertisements, in one of those jingles you just can't shake out of your head, proclaimed that Walker's watermelons were "thumpin' good."

During *The Cas Walker Farm and Home Hour* on Knoxville's radio station WROL, Walker read his own advertisements out of the newspaper. He continued the annoying practice when he moved to early-morning live television.

Walker published his own newspaper, *The Watchdog*, and regularly ran photographs of customers who had written him bad checks.

His style of rough-and-tumble, populist politics hearkened back to the nineteenth-century frontier. In their book *Knoxville, Tennessee: Continuity and Change in an Appalachian City*, Mike McDonald and Bruce Wheeler describe one of Walker's favorite antics during his races for the city council:

Cas Walker poses with a stuffed raccoon, before paintings of the gravestones of his deceased coon dogs. *Knoxville News-Sentinel photo.*

"Campaigning against the bootleg joints and 'rough places' that flour-ished in the dry city, Walker arranged to have coteries of drunks loiter about his opponent's headquarters on polling day; in his own vicinity were numerous Appalachian versions of Shirley Temple, dressed in white pinafores and wearing blue ribbons emblazoned 'Vote for my Uncle Cas.'"

Walker's most notorious stunt occurred in the middle of a city council meeting on March 6, 1956, when he instigated a fist fight with former buddy Jim Cooper over the peanut and popcorn concessions at Knoxville's Chilhowee Park. The photograph, complete with clenched teeth and cocked fist, was published in *Life* magazine. References were still being made to the incident well into the 1970s and early 1980s as Knoxville's boosters were lining up support for a World's Fair, which Walker vehemently and vocally opposed.

Walker once described his political orientation as being "agin' anything," meaning he stood firm against ideas and causes that smacked of progressivism. The concept of metro government drew his ire, as did the move to fluoridate the city's water, labeled by Walker as a plot by the Communist party.

Be it political tirade or grocery-business hucksterism, Cas's opening line was most always, "Say, neighbors," delivered in that unforgettable sandpaper voice.

Southwest Virginia secured several Cas Walker Supermarkets, primarily through the work of another of the region's most colorful characters, Virgil Q. Wacks. A native of St. Charles, Virginia, Wacks was once a minor-league baseball commissioner, mayor, owner of a block company, and county fair director. He recruited many businesses to the region as president of the Lee County Chamber of Commerce.

But Wacks was best known for his variety show that ran on regional television. Over a period of twenty-five years this graduate in cinematography from the New York School of Photography would document grand openings and ribbon cuttings all across Southern Appalachia with his Super 8 movie camera and narrate them for TV. It was Wacks who convinced Walker to open stores in the Southwest Virginia area.

Cas Walker's life intersected with my own family's in two curious ways. He wisely convinced my cousins Carl and J. P. Sauceman, who played country music on his radio show in the late 1940s, to stop calling their band "The Hillbilly Ramblers" and opt for "The Green Valley Boys" instead.

Then, in the early 1980s, my wife Jill taught pre-employment training behind the wall at Brushy Mountain State Penitentiary in Petros, Tennessee. Inmates who took the class had to secure a job on the outside before being released for parole. Cas Walker stepped forward and gave these men a job and a second chance.

Cas Walker's politics could be as irritating as his voice, but he never missed an opportunity to help others realize a better life. Cas died in 1998, but his memory is very much alive in the mind of fellow Sevier Countian Dolly Parton, who got her first professional gig in 1956, when she was just ten years old, on *The Cas Walker Farm and Home Hour.*

Walker was asked one time if he had ever made a mistake. "Yeah, I've made a lot of them," he shot back. "I fired the Everly Brothers. I told them rock and roll wouldn't sell groceries. Look where they went to."

"Urpsies and Burpsies"

The Legacy of Arnold Zandi

Yelling "Hot dogs, cold drinks!" was too dull and ordinary for Arnold J. "Burpsy" Zandi. For nearly fifty years he trudged the steps of the University of Tennessee's Neyland Stadium, calling out, "Urpsies and Burpsies and Yummies for the tummy!"

Zandi probably sold more hot dogs than anyone in East Tennessee before his retirement in 1993. He died one year later.

Zandi ran for about every political office he could think of, always enthusiastically, always unsuccessfully. He campaigned for Knoxville City

Arnold Zandi, in statuesque, Olympian pose, prepares to charge up the steps at Neyland Stadium during the University of Tennessee-Mississippi State football game, September 13, 1986. *Knoxville News-Sentinel photo.*

Council, mayor, governor of Tennessee, the United States Senate, and even President of the United States.

His son Jackie told the *Knoxville News-Sentinel* there were three factors you could always count on when Zandi ran for something: he always ran as an independent, he never accepted campaign contributions, and he always lost.

"He believed that money is what causes problems for politicians," Jackie said. "If people give a large contribution, they expect something back. He believed in running for the people and not for the politics."

My first memory of "Burpsy" goes back to the middle 1960s, when the University of Tennessee basketball team played in an old refurbished armory, the Stokely Athletics Center. Coach Ray Mears's players put on a choreographed pre-game show back then, twirling orange and white basketballs and riding unicycles. Zandi's agility and antics were just as entertaining.

Well into his eighties, with a heavy tray of hot dogs and soft drinks suspended from his neck on a towel-wrapped tether, Zandi covered acres of territory in one of the country's largest football stadiums. He kept the job long enough to hawk dogs during basketball games in the university's spacious Thompson-Boling Arena.

Buying a hot dog from Arnold "Burpsy" Zandi afforded Volunteer fans a brief brush with one of the South's most vibrant personalities—and a little for the tummy to boot.

Pizza, Bitte

Mama Mia's Pizza, Kingston, Tennessee

"Most of them, they think I'm nuts if I tell them try a sauerkraut pizza, and then they like it. It tastes good with sausage, with pepperoni, with ham. Sauerkraut pizza is good."

Lottie O'Brien was born in Bavaria, married an Irishman named William O'Brien, and makes Italian pizza in the East Tennessee lakeside community of Kingston. Mama Mia's, the sign proclaims, is "famous since 1971."

Before she emigrated from Augsburg, Germany as a war bride in 1950, Lieselotte had never even heard of pizza. She learned the art of pizza-making in the U. S. from her Italian mother-in-law Dorothy Caccia.

Lottie's husband was a job shopper for the Tennessee Valley Authority. He'd have a job for six months, and when it was completed he'd have to travel on.

"Every time he had a job, I had a kid. I had eight kids."

Not only does Lottie make her own pizza dough and five-hour French bread for sandwiches, every two weeks she makes 50 pounds of sausage.

"I don't believe to buy all that stuff. I make it from scratch, my sausage. It's made of pork and you put in all the ingredients the Italians do, the fennel seeds, the sage, bread crumbs, whatever I get ahold of."

Lottie's pizza sauce is homemade, too, an uncooked combination of whole tomatoes, oregano, garlic, and crushed red peppers. The sauce for her spaghetti, lasagna, and meatball sandwiches, however, cooks ten hours in a stock pot set in a water pan. It's the same length of time she takes to roast the beef for her subs.

The pizza is baked on cornmeal in an irreplaceable, antique Blake brick oven brought down from New York.

"I never get out of the kitchen," Lottie tells me, as she nears eighty. "I come in the morning at 10 o'clock and stay here until 10 or 11, every day, for thirty-four years. I have the German touch, too, not just Italian. I just do it my way. My way or no way. How about that? I'm not changing. I'm too old for changing."

German-born Lottie O'Brien makes
Italian Pizza in Roane County, Tennessee.
Photo by Fred Sauceman.

Mama Mia's Pizza
705 West Race Street
Kingston, Tennessee
(865) 376-5050

A Taste from 1926

Ale-8-One, Winchester, Kentucky

Soft drinks were invented in the South, and the region still leads the nation in their consumption. The top ten soft-drinking states are all below the Mason-Dixon Line. While many of the Dixie-born brands went national over the years, Ale-8-One has remained a regional refresher. At the bottling plant in Winchester, Kentucky, the formula for the ginger-flavored beverage has been a family secret for over eighty years.

Say the name quickly and you get a hint about its origin: Ale-8-One. When the drink was invented in 1926 by George Lee Wainscott, his company had already been in business for twenty-four years, making a cola that attempted to compete with the big boys in the market. Unable to come up with a name he liked for his new drink, Wainscott asked for ideas at the Clark County Fair. The winning entry was from a fourteen-year-old girl, whose name has been lost to time. She submitted "A Late One," to describe the latest thing in soft drinks.

"Wainscott punned that down to the play on words, Ale-8-One. And that's what it's stayed ever since," says Wainscott's great-great-nephew Fielding Rogers, now executive vice president of the Ale-8-One Bottling Company.

The business has remained in the same family since 1902, and with the exception of the addition of a diet version in 2003, Ale-8-One hasn't changed since its introduction in the Roaring Twenties.

"Usually I describe it as like a ginger ale but with a lot more flavor," says Fielding. "Some people remark that it has kind of a fruity twist, but it certainly has a lot more bite than just a ginger ale. It's got caffeine in it, which gives it a bit more flavor, and it has different carbonation levels, which I think gives it a lot more taste than normal ginger ale."

Whereas most of the soft drink industry has converted to plastic and metal, Ale-8-One has kept the tradition of selling returnable glass bottles, trucked around central and eastern Kentucky in wooden crates.

Ale-8 bottles ready to ship. *Photo by Fred Sauceman*

"The returnable bottles still make up about a quarter of our sales through this plant," says Fielding, who has a business degree from Washington and Lee University. "The customers really like the bottle. There's a 30-cent deposit on the bottle, and it's really just kind of an icon associated with Ale-8. A lot of people will swear that the returnable's the best-tasting Ale-8. But the returnable bottle and the non-returnable bottle are made by the same company with the same glass, filled with the same machinery, so I think they taste just the same."

In-store sales, up to now, are limited to Kentucky, a stretch of southern Ohio, and a piece of southern Indiana. Still, the company sells about a million and a half cases a year.

"We ship Ale-8 anywhere in the world via UPS. We have Internet sales on Ale-8-One.com, and people all over the world will order Ale-8, and right now we're sending quite a few cases per month to troops in Afghanistan and Iraq."

Ale-8-One is flavored with natural ginger. In the 1920s, Wainscott traveled all over Northern Europe, where he acquired ginger-blended recipes for experimentation. Just as important for the blending of the drink is the purity of the water. It's Winchester city water, but it's filtered through a complex cleansing system to remove any traces of chlorine.

The Rogers family is as obsessed with water purity as are the state's distillers, and Fielding notes that Kentuckians are especially partial to the marriage of Ale-8 and Bourbon. In the Rogers household, Ale-8's mixed into waffle and French toast batter as well as the family recipe for chili.

"We really take a normal chili recipe with ground sausage, ground beef, beans, and then anytime we have cans with either beans or tomato paste, or tomato sauce, we just rinse the cans out with Ale-8 and then pour it in the chili pot and simmer it down. It just gives it a different kind of flavor that you wouldn't normally expect with chili. I think the ginger cooks in there really well."

Whether cooked into a pot of chili in the fall or quaffed on a hot day in July or August when sales are at their peak, the fizzy, green-bottled product has become known as Kentucky's soft drink. But the Rogers family is now negotiating with distributors to spread the drink's fruity ginger flavor and its eighty-year history beyond the borders of the Bluegrass State.

Ale-8-One Bottling Company
25 Carol Road
Winchester, Kentucky
(859) 744-3484

Tamale Talk

Mary's Hot Tamales, Knoxville, Tennessee

In the 1930s and 1940s, wobbly tamale carts were common sights on the streets of Appalachian cities. With the influx of Mexican immigrants, corn-husked tamales are familiar fare in the region today. A rarer find is the Mississippi Delta-style tamale, ground beef wrapped in seasoned commercial cornmeal and steamed in paper. Clara Robinson ate them as a girl in Greenville, Mississippi, and, following the pattern so common among African-Americans during the era of Jim Crow segregation, she left her home on the banks of the Mississippi River for work in Chicago. Pursuing higher education at Knoxville College, her sister Mary Manuel settled in the hills of East Tennessee, where she later started a business making Deep South hot tamales. When Mary died, Clara, now a great-grandmother, took over the business.

Fred Sauceman: Tell me how you all got from Greenville, Mississippi, to Knoxville, Tennessee, how that occurred.

Clara Robinson: Growing up, my sister and I started school together and we ended up together, we graduated together. I was older, but they wouldn't let me start school until she got ready to go. So, we finished school in 1960, from Coleman High School in Greenville, Mississippi. She decided to come to Knoxville to go to school. I got married and moved to Chicago with my family. The kids all got grown and gone, and my sister decided she liked it here and was going to stay here, so I came to visit. Visiting her here, I liked Knoxville, so I decided to move to Knoxville to live. That was in 1988. My sister, we were friends of the hot tamale man in Greenville, Mississippi, Charlie Greene, and he was the hot tamale man here, too. He decided he was going to retire, getting old and want to retire, so he felt that we might could take over the business. He felt that we could do well with it, and so far, we did. My sister started it back in '89. She died in 2000, and to this point, I'm just trying to carry on.

FS: Now, she was in public school work.

CR: Mary was a public school worker. She was a truant attendant. I think she taught elementary education when she first got out of school. But then she didn't like classroom so she went into the truancy. And she was in there for twenty-five years. She still worked up until the month before she died. Mary got sick but I didn't know she was sick. She was ill, but she never did tell me. She died within a month after I took her to the hospital. The burden was on me. Now I'm saying, "Lord, can I handle it?" I'm not a business person. Mary was the business part of this deal, in every way. But so far, I haven't done too bad.

FS: Why was it important to you to keep her name on the business?

CR: Because she was the business. As a matter of fact, she is the business. Everybody know Mary's. I just couldn't very well change it to Clara. They'd say, "Well, who's Clara?" Mary was the business, and I felt that I owed it as a tribute to her to leave it as Mary's.

FS: Did she have a family?

CR: Nobody but Mary. She helped me with mine. She never got married, never had children. None of that.

FS: Tell me about eating tamales in the Delta when you all were growing up and how common they were.

CR: All we knew was tamales. We never questioned what was in them or anything. All we know, we liked them. Growing up in Mississippi back in those days, back in the '50s and '60s, we didn't have anything. We survived, but we didn't consider ourselves as no rich folks. But tamales was a delicacy for us, 'cause we couldn't wait for Saturdays. We couldn't get but three. I think they were something like 10 or 15 cents then. So we couldn't wait to get us three tamales. We'd have enough money to get three, and we'd go home and eat them and enjoy them, and we couldn't wait for Saturday to come again and eat some more. But they were plentiful down there.

FS: Where would you buy them in Greenville back then?

CR: We lived on a street called Cleveland Street, and on the next corner, a couple of blocks up, it was called Nelson Street, and this man had this little house, little bitty house, just he could fit in it with his hot tamale bucket,

Clara Robinson. *Photo by Larry Smith.*

and that's where we would walk the two blocks to the corner to get our tamales.

FS: Do you remember when you made your first tamale?

CR: Yeah, we made our first tamale in my kitchen when I moved here. She didn't start this business 'til I got here. We made the first tamale in my kitchen. I was living on Brown Avenue in Knoxville. We opened the business in August, it had to be around the first week of August, 1989, that's when we made our first tamale. Mr. Greene was right there with us to see us through it all. We made them, and he would go out and sell them. With his little pushcart, he would go out and sell them. That's how we got started.

FS: Describe for me how you make a tamale.

CR: Of course you know I use beef, ground beef, with my seasonings, which is a secret, as we all know. I make my own meal. Now some people uses this whatever it is that they sell in the stores, but I make my meal myself from Three Rivers meal. I make my own meal, and I make it as a paste. It stays on that paper. Of course, we use hot tamale paper. I season it up and everything, what I think's supposed to go in it. We spread it out so far on that paper, and then I make up my meat with what I put in it, and then we put it in that paper and roll it. And we've been hand-rolling it ever since we started.

FS: And then you steam it?

CR: Okay, of course your meal is already half-done anyway because you have to use that with hot water, so what we do, once we get it rolled, the meat is done because of course I had to cook the meat, so you just put it in a pot, steam them up in water, and then I put a sauce over them.

FS: How long do they steam?

CR: Oh well, when they start boiling real good, then you got to lower your heat and let them kind of settle back down. I usually do them about an hour.

FS: Describe the sauce.

CR: Oh it's just a tomato sauce I put on them with seasonings, and I pours it and covers the whole pot of tamales. And then once they finish cooking, then they start settling down.

FS: When we got them for takeout, you put in little packages of Texas Pete Hot Sauce. Any particular reason you use Texas Pete?

CR: No, you know, we started out with Texas Pete. I don't know why. I could use any kind, I guess, but that's the only kind I really have found in the little packs. And I usually buy my supplies at Hackney's, so I just get whatever they have there, and my little Styrofoam containers. Now people do sit and eat here if they're in a hurry to go to work, but now it's carry-out because we have only one entrance, so if anything happens, something happened around here, how's all these people going to get out if they all sitting in here eating in this little small space? So this is why it's carry-out.

FS: How did Mary pick this spot?

CR: You know, that I don't know, but when I first moved here, I got my hair done here, in this same little space. It was a beauty shop. So the lady decided she wanted to expand, and Mary said, "Clara, you know that might be ideal for our little tamale shop." And then there it is. We got our plumbers in and our electricians and we got everything set up, and it worked out fine. I think it's big enough.

FS: Tell me about this vegetarian tamale you have listed on the wall.

CR: I got this one particular customer, he used to come in all the time, "Clara, why don't you sell vegetarian tamales?" Now what is a vegetarian tamale? This I'm asking him. He say it's a tamale that has no real meat, he say. You know, beef and stuff. So I told him, I said, "Well, I'll give it a try. You reckon it'll sell?" And he said, "I tell you what. I'll supply all your needs for the first batch." And he did. And you know, the vegetarian tamale comes with that soybean stuff, well, you know, it's grainy, but once you mix it up, it looks just like meat. But it's not meat. With me seasoning it up the way it's supposed to be, you can't hardly tell the difference. I know the difference, but the other people can't. So it's made more or less out of whatever vegetarians eat.

FS: What do people say about your tamales other than me telling you they're the best Delta-style tamales we've ever had?

CR: They say they're good, and then they say, "How did you get into tamales? You don't look Mexican." I say, "Well, I don't think so, you know." But it's a product, it's a food, and if you find something that people eat, why not? And I think we've done well with it, going over with it, you know. I've had them to come in and tell me that they've tried all kinds, but they end up back here. Because some people look for cheaper prices.

FS: What did you do right after graduation from high school?

CR: In 1962, I got married. My husband he was in the Air Force, and it didn't work, and my uncles would come down to visit because at that time my grandparents were alive, and they all lived there together, and they told us we could make it in Chicago. You could find a good job and make good wages, so that's why we went to Chicago.

FS: Your husband's first name was?

CR: Candosey.

FS: That's an unusual name. Where'd it come from?

CR: Who knows? But his father was named Candosey. And I never know where they got it from, but he was a junior.

FS: Did he take a job in Chicago, and did you take a job in Chicago?

CR: Oh, yes. I went to Chicago, and right off the bat, you could go into the hospitals and work as a nurse's aide. Or in the dietary department, so I started out in the dietary department. And then I worked my way on up to a nurse's aide. At that time you didn't have to be certified, so I went from dietary to patient care.

FS: What did your husband do?

CR: Odd jobs. He was never really one to hold down a job. They would take him out to the steel mills and things to work. Then my husband died, so it's me and the children now, and it wasn't easy, but I made it. I had three kids, two boys and a girl, and I lost my oldest son at nineteen. He was in a car accident. The other kids, they got grown, and I basically got tired of the cold weather in Chicago, and my sister was here and I liked it here, so I decided to move here, to Knoxville.

FS: What else do you serve here besides tamales?

CR: I sell the little chicken dish there, chicken fajitas, over rice, now that's a chopped chicken in a fajita sauce served over rice. And I sell hot dogs and bologna. I even sell chicken wings. I fry wings, but I fry them by order. And I make my own little sweet potato tart, that's the little pie you can buy.

FS: Describe those.

CR: Well, it's just a little sweet potato batter. I puts it in a little shell I buy. You might see them in the store sometime. Pecan pies, and little bitty pies. But that's what they are.

FS: Homemade?

CR: Homemade. I do it all from scratch.

FS: Is the spicing in there like a sweet potato pie?

CR: Oh yeah, and I even have orders for big pies during the holidays. I got customers they want the 9-inch pies that I prepare for them. I do those only by order, but I keep the little ones on hand all the time.

Mary's Hot Tamales
1931 East Magnolia Avenue
Knoxville, Tennessee
(865) 637-2033

Venerating Greasy Beans and Sweet Cheeks

Davidson's Country Store and Farm, Rogersville, Tennessee

When he got big enough to feed himself, Will Davidson would grab fresh green beans with both fists and eat them like most children consume French fries. If his mother was in a hurry and resorted to warming up a can of beans, young Will detected the substitution immediately and left the flavorless pile on his plate.

Will comes from a long line of green bean eaters and growers. His great-great-grandfather bought the land that Will, his sister Katie, and their parents Bill, Jr., and Debbie farm today near Surgoinsville, Tennessee. M. S. Looney opened a store on the property in 1902, and families traded there until the business fell victim to the Great Depression.

Bill, Jr., and Debbie still have the old ledgers, with records of chicken trades, sugar purchases, and potato swaps going back to 1906. Dinsmores, Prices, Leepers, and Housewrights, families that still populate the county, are represented in the handwritten columns. J. F. Goodson, founder of the JFG coffee company, was an occasional customer. M. S. Looney would trade just about anything for a chicken, which was as good as cash back then.

The store stood empty and served as a storehouse for hay until the Davidsons decided to refurbish it about five years ago. They had been selling vegetables from their farm across the road in a stiflingly hot tent.

Davidson's Country Store is floored and walled with North Carolina knotty pine and decorated with antiques like a Minneapolis-made egg scale and a tobacco setter.

From late April until Halloween, Davidson's bins and shelves are stocked with produce grown right across Carters Valley Road. When spring's first strawberries come in, the store opens, and when the last pumpkin's sold, it closes for the winter.

Bill Davidson, Jr., passes down the lessons of the cornfield to his son Will.
Photo by Larry Smith

Will and Katie live by the rhythm of the seasons. They don't talk much about Playstations or iPods. They think about Carolina Gold raspberries and vines of purple seedless grapes. These young children understand that food doesn't originate in frosty aluminum trays or spring fully formed from drive-through windows.

Just the name of Will's favorite summer vegetable can elicit "yucks" from uninitiated classmates at Surgoinsville Middle School when he tells them he's eating Turkey Craws, an heirloom green bean. His dad grows a quarter-acre of them and says the name came from an old story about a farmer shooting a turkey and finding that bean in its gizzard. When they get to be shellies, Bill, Jr., says, the beans look like turkey eggs.

The Davidsons plant an acre and a half of half-runners each year and a quarter-acre of cornfield beans. The largest percentage of their bean plot, though, is devoted to the greasy bean, some 3 acres.

Named for their oily, shiny appearance compared to the duller half-runner, greasy beans are among the most difficult heirloom beans to grow.

They're more susceptible to environmental change and haven't been worked by plant geneticists. When it gets above 70 degrees at night they can abort their blooms. They're a mountain bean and don't take to hot weather. During one hot spell the Davidsons' plants lost 2 feet of blossoms. Bill, Jr., says this is the bean that the true green-bean connoisseur goes for.

The Davidsons drive 8-foot-long wooden stakes 2 feet into the ground every 10 feet and weave butcher's twine into a trellis pattern for the beans to run on. By the first of August they've already climbed to the top and are heading back toward the ground. Greasy beans usually sell for about 25 cents higher per pound than the other varieties, since the yield per acre is smaller.

Bill's mother Louise says her family prefers their green beans well done. She cooks them with a small amount of water, salt, cooking oil, and a chicken bouillon cube.

On land formerly devoted only to beef cattle and tobacco, the family now produces grapes, strawberries, raspberries, blackberries, beans, corn, watermelons, and cantaloupes. This year Bill is experimenting with a fall-fruiting strawberry. The seedless table grapes now grown at Davidson's Farm have undergone twenty years of research work at the University of Arkansas to make them cold-hardy.

Produce that isn't sold fresh in the store is made into jams, jellies, sauces, and soup mixes at the Clinch-Powell Community Kitchens in the Treadway community of Hancock County. Recently the Davidsons bought a revolving frozen drink dispenser from Italy, and they're turning strawberries and raspberries into refreshing, icy ciders—another way, Bill, Jr., says, of adding value to the crop.

You've heard the stories of summertime sprints from cornfield to kitchen to get the just-shucked Silver Queen and Peaches and Cream into boiling water before the precious sugar turns to a dull starch. Never mind that a few silks were still stuck between the white and yellow rows. The corn needed to be dunked into the pot as quick as the shucks came off, since the flavor loss started right when the ear was cracked off the stalk.

I remember the Silver Queen seventies, when we thought that variety was the best thing since, well, Squeeze Parkay. Word that the corn was "in" spread like a flood warning. It had to be picked, even by flashlight, and eaten or "put up." That happened one night, long after suppertime, and I played the "eat immediately" admonition to the hilt, gnawing across ten buttery, salt-gritted ears right before bedtime.

Although in almost every way life's gotten quicker since those days, in one respect we can slow down a little. Thanks to thirty years of study and experimentation by botanists, geneticists, and agronomists, we can walk from the field to the house and maybe even let the corn harvest sit around for a day or so. Scientists have found ways to delay that sugar-to-starch conversion.

Today's super sweets and triple sweets can hold their sugar for two or three days, and there's more tolerance for tardy pickers. Back then Silver Queen had to be picked within about a three-day window. After ripening, Sweet Cheeks, Bojangles, and Temptation, for example, can stay on the stalk about three times that long.

Now you don't have to pick the whole field at once, and out of the freezer the sugar level of today's corn is higher than the old sweet corns of twenty or thirty years ago.

Scientists have also figured out ways to make silking easier. Almost all the silk comes off in one handful with the husk, eliminating scrub-brushing and fastidious fingernail work.

Because of the varying maturation rates of the corn varieties he uses, Bill Davidson can plant several at one time and the yield will be staggered throughout the summer. The seed of sixty-eight-day Sweet Cheeks is vigorous enough to withstand the cold, wet soils of March, emerging as the first corn on the market.

Most of the corn grown at Davidson's is bi-color, homage to Peaches-and-Cream loyalists, with occasional white kernels flecking the ears at asymmetrical intervals. The corn is sold in the family store at less than 30 cents an ear.

As fall nears, the Davidsons manicure their corn maze, making sure the open space retains the shape of a football. Son Will escorts us through on a boiling August day, loses his way, and opts for a stalk-slapped shortcut back to the house and a slurp of raspberry cider at the store.

Yet there are five more plantings of corn to be harvested between now and frost. A few weeks later the mailbox on Carters Valley Road will start to fill up with seed catalogues, ears of Temptation will be tugged out of the family freezer, and the cycle will begin anew.

Davidson's Country Store
and Farm
1006 Carters Valley Road
Rogersville, Tennessee
(423) 345-3384

Roan Mountain Corn Gravy

Margaret Propst (1915-2005) inherited this heirloom recipe from her mother, the late Florence Graybeal of Roan Mountain in Carter County, Tennessee. Mrs. Propst taught home economics for seventeen years at Cloudland High School, but when the male teachers went overseas during World War II she added chemistry, history, and English to her repertoire. When Cherokee Dam was being built in East Tennessee, Mrs. Propst taught rural housewives how to use new pressure-canning equipment just on the market. She also offered food and nutrition instruction, teaching residents how to eat well and stay well. She completed her professional career as a home demonstration agent for eighteen years in Greene County, Tennessee. She served corn gravy for breakfast, lunch, and dinner and preferred white corn, such as Silver Queen, although she occasionally fell back on yellow or even canned.

Roan Mountain Corn Gravy

4 ears corn
2/3 cup water
2 tablespoons sugar
1/2 teaspoon salt
1/4 teaspoon black or white pepper
2 tablespoons butter
4 1/2 cups milk (In the mountains we call it "sweet" milk.)
2 tablespoons flour
1/2 cup cold water

Cut the corn off of each ear and scrape the cob. Place corn in a saucepan with 2/3 cup water, sugar, salt, pepper, and butter. Cook for at least five minutes or until corn is fully done. Add milk and heat until boiling point is reached. In a separate bowl dissolve flour into 1/2 cup cold water and mix until smooth. Add this mixture slowly to the boiling corn and cook five to ten minutes or until the flour taste is gone. Watch to ensure that the corn does not boil over. Stir constantly while mixture is boiling. This should be slightly thick but not as thick as cream-style gravy would be. Corn gravy is best served on top of freshly baked biscuits.

Margaret Propst. *Courtesy the Propst family.*

2

Baklava in Beanland: Immigrant Influences in Appalachia

We quaff Cokes from flower vases,
heed Judaic judgments on saltines,
salvage sauce, and eschew ham.

Rose Bowl Steers Greeks Toward Steaks

The Peerless Restaurant, Johnson City, Tennessee

"Beautiful taste buds." It's Peerless owner Jim Kalogeros's answer to my question about why Greeks have done so well in the restaurant business in the South. In most every medium to large Southern city you'll find at least one Greek-owned eatery.

The owners may be Greek, but other than a crunchy spinach pastry appetizer and honey-sweetened baklava for dessert, most of their menus show little connection to the homeland. Instead, they are eclectic American. John's in Birmingham, Alabama, serves some of the South's best cornbread. The Bright Star in nearby Bessemer features a gumbo that would be right at home on any Louisiana table. The Mayflower in Jackson, Mississippi, plates up Tex-Mex enchiladas with chili and cheese. And the Regas in Knoxville, Tennessee, may well be a world leader in sales of red velvet cake.

At The Peerless in Johnson City, Tennessee, the reputation is built on beef from the American Midwest. But it didn't start out that way. Greek immigrant John Kalogeros opened a barbecue house in 1938, choosing Johnson City mainly because he'd learned that the veterans at the Mountain Home hospital had been given a $100 bonus. With a growing college and busy railroads, John figured Johnson City held the ticket to a secure future for his family. He was right.

John quickly learned the art of Southern barbecue and mixed a mountain-style sauce dominated by tomatoes and sorghum. In 1940, though, a friendly wager changed the course of his business and forever altered eating habits in the Tri-Cities.

Other than an occasional coaching change, rarely does much good come from a University of Tennessee gridiron loss. The year 1940 was an exception. The Volunteers were shut out by the University of Southern California Trojans in the Rose Bowl that year, after the Vols had not been scored on during the 1939 regular season. Thinking that the odds were highly in his favor, John bet on Tennessee but lost. His penalty: he had to cook steak

Jim Kalogeros and his family have been serving steaks for over 60 years. *Photo by Larry Smith.*

dinners for his friends, who quickly spread the word about his skill with a cut of beef. Soon diners from all over town were coming in for 75-cent steaks. Today, The Peerless ranks as one of the region's premier steakhouses.

The North Roan Street institution is presided over by John's son Jim. For his eightieth birthday a few years ago Jim was given a new water ski vest, which he still uses today, gliding along behind his boat on Boone Lake—that is, when he's not putting in 12-hour days at the restaurant.

Preparation starts in the Peerless kitchen at 2 P.M., and Jim has already been at work for three hours. He stands in the restaurant's front entryway like a traffic cop, sending a produce supplier back to the kitchen with a box of red and yellow tomatoes and a plumber in the other direction to unstop a drain. He fields phone calls, refuses to take reservations, inspects a 1 1/2-pound super colossal yellow onion soon to be sliced into rings for one of the restaurant's most popular appetizers, and makes sure bowls for his famous Greek salad are chilled to the right temperature.

The kitchen is a model of efficiency and frugality. A sign near the salad station reads, "Only one anchovy per salad. If the guest wants extra, you must charge for extra (very expensive)." Alongside is a magazine clipping: "American Airlines saved $40,000 in 1987 by eliminating one olive from each salad served in first-class."

In another posted communication, wait staff are urged to adhere to the "No Lag Theory" and time their placement of orders accordingly.

No matter whether you're there for steak, fried shrimp, or chicken covered with the original 1938 recipe barbecue sauce, what you'll see first on the table is a tray of saltine crackers and a saucer with two mounds of butter. It's a restaurant trademark, and one Jim Kalogeros intends never to change. He says a group of Jewish New York executives, visiting the Bemberg and North American Rayon plants in Elizabethton, begged him never to get rid of the saltines, and he won't, although he has added a long, rectangular multi-grain cracker to the tray.

Ask diners what they like best about Peerless Greek salads and they'll most likely say feta cheese and peas. About 6,000 pounds of feta are sprinkled on salads each year, and the peas were Jim's father's idea. "Daddy started the peas. Children love peas," says Jim.

No seasoning is added to Peerless steaks. They're cooked on a shiny metal grill in beef fat. "I buy the very best beef available and do as little to it as possible," Jim declares.

When I took novelist William Styron to The Peerless in 1997, he told me he'd never had a better steak, even in New York City. Another of my best Peerless memories is seeing the late CBS newsman Eric Sevareid devour a nearly rare Black Angus T-bone only a couple of hours before he gave a public lecture at East Tennessee State University in 1990.

The Peerless has always attracted the famous. Photographs of Bob Hope, Bob Barker, Tom Jones, and Red Skelton hang just inside the entryway. In the 1960s, when the administration of ETSU feared what poet Allen Ginsberg might say on campus and turned him away, he held court in one of the banquet rooms at The Peerless, with students and faculty seated cross-legged around him on the floor as he spoke and read poetry.

The forty-five-year-old fiberglass black bull out front has been treated to a number of indignities over the years—painted hog pink one time, dressed in brassiere and panties in preparation for the visit of singer Tom Jones in the 1970s, and nearly kidnapped once before the Kalogeros family rescued it. As one of Johnson City's most unforgettable icons, it's a subject for memory book photographs for diners of all ages.

The Peerless Restaurant
2531 North Roan Street
Johnson City, Tennessee
(423) 282-2351

Mall Food di Napoli
Italian Village, Kingsport, Tennessee

Long after the mall walkers have put away their Reeboks, when the lights of the arcade no longer blink and carts selling "lucky bamboo" are covered over, the pizza ovens at Italian Village continue to glow. They stay on all night to maintain constant and correct temperatures for thick-crusted, square Sicilian pizza and thin-crusted, round Neapolitan.

I discovered Italian Village just days after it opened in the Fort Henry Mall over twenty-five years ago when I took a job as a reporter for WKPT television. In its heyday, WKPT not only gave me rich broadcasting experience, but it also opened up a host of new dining possibilities, since television personnel weren't quite as obsessed with their weight in 1978 as they are today.

Enter the Steak Special. Diminutive versions of this sandwich now appear on restaurant menus all over the Tri-Cities, but the Italian Village original is still the best and biggest. Sliced sirloin is chopped and tossed on a grill with pepperoni, Italian sausage, green peppers, mushrooms, onions, provolone cheese, and a tomato sauce that has simmered for five hours. The restaurant rings with the metal-on-metal din created as cooks wield turners in rhythmic fashion, swipe them across the grill, and shovel the smoking blend onto a bun. Owner Raffaele Misciagna calls it a "good combination, one of my favorites." In his native Italian, he exclaims, "*Si sposa*"—it marries.

Raffaele says the Steak Special sandwich he now serves had its origin on Long Island, New York, where he worked at a restaurant called Umberto's after emigrating at age thirteen to the United States from his home near the Adriatic Sea in Southern Italy.

Raffaele and his brothers Ricardo and Michael came to Kingsport with almost nothing. Now they operate three restaurants: Italian Village, Raffaele's, and Giuseppe's.

"We struggled and worked without paying ourselves. Now, after almost twenty-five years, we can allow ourselves an extra day off or even a vacation."

Joe Gobster and Chris Dettor slide out a Neapolitan at the Italian Village. *Photo by Larry Smith.*

Stone, wood, and iron are the elemental requirements for pizza baking at Italian Village. Cooks form Neapolitan pizzas on wooden paddles and slide them onto stones in the restaurant's three ovens. For the Sicilian or thicker-crusted pizzas, dough is placed in black iron pans and allowed to rise. In both cases the dough is aged at least twenty-four hours.

"In America we eat pizza morning until night," says Raffaele. "In Italy, we entertain with pizza in the evenings."

Pizza is available by the slice at Italian Village, which works well with mall traffic since some customers come in for only one slice between meals. Since he can't sell pizza on the sidewalk like he could in New York, a mall location is the next best thing.

When I asked Raffaele what makes a good tomato sauce, he fired back an instant answer: simplicity. The pizza sauce isn't even cooked. It's a combination of tomatoes, olive oil, and fresh basil, the Southern Italian staples he grew up eating.

In the early days of the business, fresh basil was so rare in East Tennessee that the Misciagnas had to grow their own.

Sauces are made every other day—the traditional Italian tomato sauce; a ragú with carrots and onions; a Bolognese-style meat sauce with Parmesan cheese; and the uncooked pizza sauce.

"We come from a country of farmers and fishermen, and we stick with the old traditions," says Raffaele. "My customers say, Ralph, don't change anything. When I see third-generation customers, it's very satisfying."

Italian Village
Fort Henry Mall
Kingsport, Tennessee
(423) 247-7391

A Strip Mall Shock

Café One 11, Johnson City, Tennessee

The outside of the building is the neutral, non-descript color of sand. The sign is strip-mall style, green and white, undistinguished, rectangular. But open the door, walk through the multicolored curtain, and you enter a place of gold leaf, burnished Buddhas and leatherlike walls.

Café One 11 in Johnson City, Tennessee, is a temple of neo-Asian cuisine, next door to the offices of Weight Loss Success. The blending of chocolate martinis is overseen by a bronze Buddha from a Beijing antique shop. Realtors in Brooks Brothers sip Bellinitinis alongside guys in windbreakers swilling Michelob Ultra.

The dance floor is made of bamboo planks from Home Depot. The Sunday brunch layout is laden with simple scrambled eggs; a hot-out-of-the-wok mélange of mushrooms and chicken; a whole smoked salmon, the flesh forking off in succulent sheets; and cubes of cool mango mousse dressed with whipped cream, tiny mint leaves, and bits of fresh mango.

"Our philosophy of cooking is very visual," says co-owner Scott Hsu. "The first thing you should notice is the appearance, then the aroma, then, most importantly, the taste."

Color, texture, and design are second nature to Scott, a graphic designer, and his wife Linda, a former student at New York's Fashion Institute of Technology. East Tennesseans since 1989, this Taiwanese couple undertook the redesign of their former Hunan Park restaurant almost unaided, from using sticks to draw outlines of plants in the wet concrete floor to texturizing the walls with mocha- and espresso-colored paint.

They solicited the help of local artist Andrew Moore, who fashioned the colored light fixtures above the bar and painted a canvas of roses for the back dining room. A wedding kimono in reds and golds, interwoven with images of cranes, hangs behind the bar and a teakwood door and window reveal a rice paper scene reminiscent of an Asian temple.

Linda Hsu. *Photo by Fred Sauceman.*

Those in search of traditional Chinese cuisine can still find Scott's hot and sour soup, spiced with crushed Sichuan peppercorns, but the menu has been modified with such cross-cultural fare as an Indian tandoori-style salmon covered in a cucumber yogurt sauce common in the Greek kitchen.

The Rock and Roll is a tray of eight maki rolls stuffed with asparagus, cream cheese, and pickled gourd; topped with two types of caviar and a rock shrimp; and squirted with shots of wasabi aioli and Vietnamese firecracker sauce.

Sushi chef Tai Sheng Weng slices, shapes, and serves a full line of Japanese delicacies. "The most important part of sushi is the rice," Scott advises. "For the best balance of flavors, we use a rice from California that doesn't stick to the teeth. The length of the soaking time, the act of fanning it until it cools, and the right blending of vinegars are the secrets."

Vietnamese steak, made from a cut called "flat-top" from the upper portion of the sirloin, is citrus-marinated and pan-seared. Scott Hsu stopped bringing it to the table sizzling, though. He says dry-cleaning bills just got too expensive.

Scott, who does the cooking at the couple's other Johnson City restaurant, Café Pacific, met Linda in New York City, where he was running a restaurant on Second Avenue. Linda's uncle, Yung Fu Chiang, is a master chef in the city. He travels to various Asian restaurants making his secret sauces—kung pao, garlic, and Sichuan—as Linda says, for "big money."

Café One 11
111 Broyles Drive
Johnson City, Tennessee
(423) 283-4633

Fast-Food Adobo

The Philippine Connection, Knoxville, Tennessee

Carmelina Shelton, tiny and tobogganed, keeps three woks going all day long in a closet-sized corridor of a kitchen. On the shelf above, always within quick reach, are tall plastic containers of black peppercorns, various forms of garlic, vinegar, and soy sauce.

Those ingredients represent the coming together of Chinese and Spanish cuisines, traditions that, through trade and colonization, form the foundation of Filipino cookery. Factor in another influence, American take-out, and the result is a rarity in the Mountain South: a Filipino fast-food joint.

Aida Davison and Conchita Lyon cleaned up what was once a dump of a building and opened The Philippine Connection on Magnolia Avenue in Knoxville, Tennessee, in May of 1988.

Aida had been cooking since she was six years old, remembered her mother's techniques, and brought that knowledge to America in 1967 as an Air Force bride.

Many East Tennesseans were first introduced to Philippine adobos and sautéed noodles during the 1982 World's Fair. After the fair closed in October of that year, locals were left without a source for the sour and salty flavor combinations characteristic of this archipelago of 7,107 islands.

Situated near Chilhowee Park, The Philippine Connection shares the glaring red-and-yellow exterior coloration common to many American fast-food establishments. There are a couple of tables for dining on the premises, but the business is primarily take-out and the clientele is predominantly American.

When she first opened, Aida says customers specifically requested no garlic. "Now that we've found that it's good for your health, some of our customers demand extra, extra garlic."

Lumpia is the Filipino version of an egg roll, but longer and thinner around, almost flutelike. The wrapping is thinner, too, and produces a shattering crunch. The beef or pork filling is redolent of garlic.

Aida Davison spends her days cooking adobo and lumpia like her mother did in The Philippines.
Photo by Fred Sauceman.

Most of the wok-cooked creations at The Philippine Connection are available in small or large portions, with a choice of chicken, pork, beef, shrimp, or all four, and there's even an all-vegetable option. Small versions are plenty for hearty eaters, accompanied by plain white rice or Chinese-style fried rice and an egg roll.

If there is a national dish of The Philippines, the nod goes to adobo, a Spanish-influenced, quickly cooked "stew" seasoned with the omnipresent vinegar, soy sauce, garlic, and black pepper mixture. The Philippine Connection sells more chicken adobo than any other meat choice.

"At home, I cook it with the bones, but here there's no time—it's all boneless meat," says Aida.

Filipino cookery is also heavily dependent on noodles of various colors and textures. Headlining the menu at The Philippine Connection is *pancit guisado*, sautéed noodles.

"I do this country-style, and it's my mother's original recipe from a region outside Manila," says Aida, sporting a red sweatshirt with intertwined American and Philippine flags.

Prepared Cantonese style, the yellow-gold noodles soften in the wok after the meat and vegetables—broccoli, carrots, onions, and cabbage—are cooked.

All the adobo and noodle dishes contain a sufficient amount of meat, but the meat doesn't play a dominant role in the cuisine.

Aida describes the 16-ounce tropical drink Halo-Halo as like a milkshake or a piña colada without the alcohol. It's a cold blend of mung beans, evaporated milk, coconut gel, jackfruit, crushed ice, and shredded coconut.

The woks at The Philippine Connection stay full for eleven-hour business days Monday through Saturday, and the ladies spooning up the carry-out orders go through truckloads of Styrofoam in a week's time. But being covered up with work is what drives them, as they easily shift between their native language of The Philippines and confident English, unperturbed as customers line up from the cash register through the front door to take home tastes of the islands.

The Philippine Connection
3225 East Magnolia Avenue
Knoxville, Tennessee
(865) 522-5276

Just Say Mo

King Tut's Grill, Knoxville, Tennessee

Every Wednesday, on Egyptian Night, between bites of stuffed grape leaves and spoons of fava beans, diners at King Tut's Grill beat toy bongos, toot kazoos, and dance the Macarena under disco lights. Owner Monir Girgis shoots rubber chickens with toy guns and stuffs them in Styrofoam takeout boxes. Soft drinks are served in flower vases customers bring in from flea markets.

It's a Cairo karaoke roadhouse, run by Christian Orthodox Coptics, in the Vestal community of South Knoxville, Tennessee. Despite the mayhem and the fact that some have described the place as a "dive," the food is authentic and good and no alcohol is served.

Born in the ancient world, Mo, as he prefers to be called, caught on to modern American promotional tactics quickly. He's a master at hype and slogan repetition.

"I have best Greek salad ever" is his favorite line, followed closely by, "I recommend it highly."

When he first opened King Tut's, Mo couldn't afford newspaper advertising. So he printed up 500 T-shirts, sold them cheap, and told all the purchasers they could have free Basboosa, a baked semolina cake with honey and yogurt, until he dies.

He says his customers told him, "Mo, we will never wish you to die; we wish you always to have Basboosa."

His next limited-edition shirt, in burgundy, earned wearers free Arabic coffee for a lifetime, and on the back of the third one he printed, "Just Say Mo" and "Highly Recommended."

"People come in here and they ask me, Mo, what are we going to eat tonight, and I always tell them, so I always end all of my words with 'highly recommended,' like 'best Greek salad in Knoxville, highly recommended.'"

Whether he's topped competitors with regard to taste is subjective opinion, but he's surely beaten them with bulk. Mo's "small" Greek salad is a

Mo and Seham Girgis. *Photo by Fred Sauceman.*

pyramid of lettuce; tomato; onion; black olives; sliced eggs; a Greek dressing of olive oil, vinegar, and oregano made by his wife Seham; and grated, not crumbled, feta cheese.

"We Egyptians, we always eat some rice, a lot of vegetables, a small amount of meat like chicken or lamb, and beans, a dish called *ful madammas*, cooked on the stove like pinto beans but with a different kind of beans called favas."

Mo says he got the flower vase idea from being underserved at restaurants around the city. "Many times I ask for a small ice water or something, and they bring me a very tiny glass and it will never be enough, especially in the summertime. You see a lot of people walk in here, if they've been running or riding their bicycle, they want at least five or six glasses. So I decided to serve them in something very large. Before customers have a garage sale, they think about Mo and bring me flower vases."

Seham runs the kitchen, with their daughter Christina studying at a table close by. All the recipes for the restaurant come from Seham's mother back in Cairo—dishes like *koshari*, a mixture of rice, macaroni, lentils, basil, and rosemary, topped with tomato sauce.

The grinning Mo, within earshot of his laboring wife, says, "I recommend it highly."

King Tut's Grill
4132 Martin Mill Pike
Knoxville, Tennessee
(865) 573-6021

Notes from the Red Velvet Cake Capital of the World

The Regas, Knoxville, Tennessee

Regas. The name has meant elegant dining in East Tennessee for nearly ninety years. It's one letter away from regal, which is what guests feel like from the moment they walk up to Hazel Schmid and ask for a table.

"Are you celebrating anything this evening?" asks Hazel. If it's your birthday or anniversary, she puts a star on your place card.

Frank and George Regas, immigrants from Patras, Greece, opened the restaurant on Gay Street in Knoxville, Tennessee, on July 7, 1919, first as a stool-and-counter establishment, with a few tables and booths.

Location, which later became a watchword for modern-day corporate America, led the Regas brothers to this spot alongside the Southern Railroad tracks, adjacent to the five-story Watauga Hotel and the Hotel Atkin, the finest in town before construction of the Andrew Johnson and the Farragut.

"My mother and father [Frank] had their wedding in the dining room of the Atkin," says Bill Regas.

The family later demolished the old hotel to build a 177-space parking lot. Although it was painful for the Regas kin to see the old structure collapse, the availability of that much parking kept the restaurant downtown, at its original location.

"It's unusual for a downtown restaurant to have this much parking," says Bill, a former President of the National Restaurant Association. "Lack of parking is often the reason for failure in the business. We have the character of a suburban restaurant, but we're centrally located."

As the restaurant grew, it took over the old Watauga. You can still see the hotel's brick exterior wall in the Gathering Place, the restaurant's stylish bar.

The Southern Bell Telephone Company soon set up switchboards nearby. Radio station WIVK sent its signal across the hills and valleys from studios across the street, attracting country music acts from all over the nation. The Regas eventually grew from 50-cent sizzling steaks and blue-plate specials to white tablecloths and wine lists.

Mike Connor, Hazel Schmid, and Bill Regas celebrate Hazel's fiftieth anniversary with The Regas in 2004. *Photo by Fred Sauceman.*

University of Tennessee football coach General Robert Neyland ate there. So did Franklin D. Roosevelt. The glittering Liberace dined at The Regas every time he pounded a piano in the area. Hazel, who celebrated fifty years as a Regas employee in 2004, recalls recognizing country crooner Porter Waggoner even without his rhinestones and fringe.

For generations of diners, The Regas means memory. A sixteen-year-old girl recently came back to visit Bill Regas, who had warmed her bottle when she was about a year old as her parents had dinner.

Bill remembers competing for tips as a counterman at his father's restaurant with Wendy's founder Dave Thomas, who had moved to Oak Ridge with his adoptive family during World War II. Thomas rode the bus to Knoxville every day. He and Bill could carry five plates on one arm.

"We're in the business of creating memories," says Bill. "To sit by the fire with a good meal and a glass of wine—we think that's one of the greatest things in life."

The biggest lunchtime seller nowadays is the baked schrod. The fish is covered with crushed Ritz crackers, lemon butter, and the restaurant's own seasoning, fragrant with oregano, which is sold at the front of the restaurant and in some Knoxville area grocery stores. Many buy it exclusively as a topping for cottage cheese or Grainger County tomatoes.

The Regas blends sophistication and simplicity. For the most special occasions of all, Bill recommends a 9-ounce New Zealand lobster tail and a 6-ounce, mesquite-grilled filet. This ultimate celebratory meal takes no stuffy name, not even surf and turf. The menu describes it directly and honestly— steak and lobster. No more need be said.

Along with a toasted-almond-topped, feta-sprinkled salad; a round, rustic loaf of warm, crackly bread; and a full bowl of sautéed button mushrooms, the memorable meal is almost complete.

At The Regas, a meal-ending piece of red velvet cake is obligatory. In fact, Regas may well be the red velvet cake capital of the world, and its influence has spread to a number of other Knoxville restaurants.

Back when The Regas was open twenty-four hours a day every day, Bobbie Wynn, the night manager, baked German chocolate, lemon pound, and Italian marble cakes after midnight. But it was her red velvet recipe that became a Regas trademark and party finale, a light chocolate cake topped with buttercream icing and scattered with red-colored coconut flakes.

Beginning with the $100 Frank Regas brought with him from Patras so long ago, this Greek immigrant family has built its reputation on classic American food—steaks, prime rib, clam chowder, strawberry shortcake.

"My dad told me to expand, remodel, and improve all you want to, but never close," says Bill Regas, beneath the fifty-year-old chandelier in the Walnut Room where the business began.

Trains no longer pour out passengers beneath Gay Street, and country tunes no longer stream out the windows from the long abandoned studios of WIVK. But the grills and ovens at The Regas are as busy as ever, safeguarding this storied spot in the gastronomic history of East Tennessee.

The Regas
318 North Gay Street NW
Knoxville, Tennessee
(865) 63-Regas

Hidden Hellenic

Milano's, Kingsport, Tennessee

"The Spaghetti a la Venice is the best spaghetti I've ever eaten," says Jim Clark, who runs Clark's Furniture just up the street from Milano's in Kingsport, Tennessee. "The food is superb here, the quantity is large, and the prices are reasonable."

Scrunched between a Sleep Zone and a fabric store, set back almost anonymously off chaotic East Stone Drive in the former location of a CiCi's Pizza, this Greek, Italian, and American restaurant is a culinary secret slowly leaking out among Tri-Cities diners.

The food is infused with the zeal of Kostadinos Apostolopoulos, cook and co-owner with his wife Elizabeth. Both of them are always on the premises, Dino slinging pizza dough in the open and immaculate kitchen while Elizabeth, with her captivating smile, greets customers out front, teaches toddlers the intricacies of the bubble gum machine, and shares fresh peppers from the garden with friends.

"I like you, baby," Dino exclaims as a one-year-old Guatemalan girl gazes at his bright face in fascination. Meanwhile her mother polishes off a plate of veal marsala.

"I swear, he could spoil anything," says server Christy Cole. "We've made some of the strangest orders, even a crustless pizza for a dieter, long before a national chain started advertising one."

As the name suggests, Milano's offers Italian dishes—lasagna, fettuccini carbonara, shrimp scampi, and chicken cacciatore baked with chunks of boneless chicken breast meat, peppers, onions, mushrooms, and marinara sauce.

Despite the multinational fare, in keeping with the owners' family heritage it was the Greek dishes I came for. In one evening I ate my way through most of the Hellenic section of the menu.

Milano's Greek salad dressing is a viscous emulsion of olive oil and vinegar, seasoned with feta cheese, chopped onions, and oregano. It stays

Elizabeth and Dino Apostolopoulos. *Photo by Larry Smith.*

where you pour it, coating cherry tomatoes, pepperoncini, kalamata olives, and even more feta sprinkled on top of the salad.

Dino, whose father was a butcher in Karpenisi, Greece, threads cubes of pork tenderloin and chicken breast meat onto wooden skewers for his *souvlaki.* The dish is marinated and broiled until slightly brown on the outside but still juicy and heady with oregano, olive oil, lemon juice, and garlic.

The *souvlaki* are served with rice tinted slightly yellow from a chicken broth boil. Lemon twists and slices are scattered on top for color contrast and, more importantly, for squeezing.

"Greeks love to squeeze lemon on meats, even if those meats have already been marinated in lemon juice," says Elizabeth.

Both the *souvlaki* dishes, as well as the gyro, a spiced and sliced mixture of beef and lamb, are served with Elizabeth's homemade *tzatziki,* a sauce of sour cream, garlic, cucumbers, and—you guessed it—more olive oil and lemon juice. The chunks of *souvlaki* are at their finest dipped into the cool and sour sauce.

Elizabeth makes her own *baklava* for dessert, the honey-soaked walnut confection flecked with cinnamon and allspice between leaves of nicely browned phyllo dough.

Every week or so, the Apostolopoulos family bakes up another Greek classic, *moussaka*, a layered eggplant dish topped with *béchamel* sauce.

Customer Marvin Graham says Dino had been begging him to search out goat butter. Marvin tracked some down on a farm in Yuma, Virginia, and brought a hunk down to Dino's kitchen.

"He browned that goat butter in a skillet and tossed cooked noodles around in it, and I couldn't believe how good it was."

Some customers submit orders as vague as "Give us something extra; be creative." They're taken aback at the pizza Dino places on the silver pedestal plate in front of them, often with toppings dripping off the sides.

Dino and Elizabeth work hard and keep long hours, but their love of the basic flavors of their native Mediterranean region and their exuberance in sharing those tastes keep these parents of grown sons lively and young.

Milano's
1409-D East Stone Drive
Kingsport, Tennessee
(423) 245-0010

Abruzzi Ingenuity Meets Grainger County Dirt

Riga's Pasta Sauce, Sneedville, Tennessee

The late Anna DeMarco Riga would have loved the scene. In a community kitchen on the north side of Clinch Mountain, in Hancock County, Tennessee, her son and grandson weigh fresh garlic, onions, parsley, and basil to make pasta sauce.

Just as Anna did before she left Italy for America in 1914, David Riga, Sr., and David Riga, Jr., use the freshest ingredients they can find. Once a month in the summertime they drive up from Knoxville, Tennessee, to the Clinch-Powell Community Kitchens in the Treadway community to wash, core, and strain the heralded Grainger County tomatoes.

On this day in the middle of August they process 700 pounds of tomatoes, which translate into 600 16-ounce jars and 150 24-ounce jars of Riga's Old World Italian Pasta Sauce, a product that was introduced to the market in May of 2004.

David, Sr., says this is the exact recipe his mother used back in the Abruzzi region of Italy over 100 years ago. She brought it with her to The Bronx when her family emigrated to New York at the beginning of World War I.

"We used to buy tomatoes from vendors who came around the neighborhood in New York," David remembers. "It took her three to four hours to make the sauce. She made it every Sunday, and she invited the whole neighborhood. The ladies would bring the food downstairs to our big back yard, and the men would bring the wine, homemade wine, and we'd eat and have a good time."

Anna made her own pasta in those days, and her son still does, mounting a broom handle over two chairs to dry the noodles just like his mother did. She taught her son how to cook lasagna when he was nine years old.

David Riga, Sr., using the dexterity he developed as a jeweler, carefully cores Grainger County tomatoes to make his mother's pasta sauce. *Photo by Fred Sauceman.*

Anna's sauce recipe has been stowed away in many suitcases over the years. From The Bronx it traveled with David, Sr., to South Florida then to Knoxville, where he and his son have settled.

In Florida, David, Jr., a builder by trade, carried on his grandmother's tradition of inviting friends over for Sunday meals, and the sauce was always the showpiece.

"You should jar this. You should sell this sauce," his friends insisted.

Once they moved to Tennessee, the Rigas contacted the Department of Agriculture and started looking for a place to process the sauce, since their home kitchen wasn't large enough to accommodate the quantities required for the marketplace.

Thus began a relationship with the Clinch-Powell Community Kitchens, a program of the Jubilee Project operated through the United Methodist church. Located in the once-abandoned Flat Gap Elementary School, the kitchen is as well appointed and well equipped as any restaurant facility around and is fully approved by the USDA. It's available twenty-four hours a day at a reasonable rent. Producers turn out garlic marinade, barbecue sauce, habanero pepper extract, blackberry jam, green hot sauce, creamed honey, and pumpkin butter—among a list of sixty different offerings a page and a half long, all using locally grown products.

The Appalachian Spring Cooperative, headquartered in an old Flat Gap classroom, markets Clinch-Powell products around the region. The cooperative helps local farmers find alternative crops to replace tobacco. Supported by federal grants, the cooperative stores both raw and finished products for farmers and provides access to bulk purchasing, a pool of member and contract labor, and professional marketing skills.

Greg Golden, a graduate of the Florida Culinary Institute who manages the Clinch-Powell Community Kitchens, describes the venture as an incubator. "When businesses get too big for us, they build their own facility or move into a larger one. We're not trying to make money, just to sustain the kitchen. Through all these products, we're bringing much-needed money into one of the poorest counties in the South."

Of all the Clinch-Powell clients, the Italians are the ones who break up the hard workday with a meal featuring their product. Despite a 40-gallon tilt braising pan and all the other slick technology, it takes the Rigas about as long to make the sauce as it did David, Sr.'s mother in the 1920s.

To avoid a lengthy disruption of operations, David, Sr., dispenses with the homemade pasta and instead boils up a pot of rotini; drains it carefully; grates his favorite cheese, locatelli, over the top; spoons on his sauce; adds more cheese; and serves the kitchen and co-op staff.

"It's like an afternoon in Rome," says business manager Jim Saunders.

In Grainger County, tomatoes are tied with beef as the number one agricultural commodity. About 500 acres of tomatoes are grown in the fields, and the county is dotted with some 500 greenhouses.

"Grainger County, being right on Cherokee Lake, just has the right climate," says extension agent Anthony Carver. "We grow several varieties of tomatoes, including Empire, Celebrity, and Mr. Stripey, on raised beds. The tomatoes are fed at the root system with nutrients and water, so we're not so dependent on the weather. And a lot of people attribute the goodness of our tomatoes to the fact that the county is in the middle of a limestone bed, which furnishes lime for the crop."

Nature and know-how converge in Grainger County. They're the same two elements Anna DeMarco Riga brought together in her Italian kitchen so many years ago, much to the delight of her son and grandson and now their customers.

Three Hundred Years of Italian Tradition—Gone in One Night

Novelist Adriana Trigiani Remembers Poached Meatballs in Norton, Virginia

The late Anthony Trigiani once reversed 300 years of his family's history as he prepared for a supper at St. Anthony's Catholic Church in Norton, Virginia. Someone had burned the tomato sauce. Spaghetti was about to be served, and Anthony had no time to follow his mother's age-old practice of browning the meatballs first.

So he formed them and plopped them into an unburned batch of sauce. Now all five of his daughters, both of his sons, and his widow, Ida Bonicelli Trigiani, prefer poached meatballs.

"It makes a really great, thick Bolognese sauce because the meat's cooking right in there," says Anthony and Ida's third child, best-selling novelist Adriana Trigiani, who has co-authored with her sister Mary Yolanda Trigiani a book of memories and recipes shaped and seasoned by their Italian-American heritage.

Cooking with My Sisters: One Hundred Years of Family Recipes, from Bari to Big Stone Gap traces this family's culinary heritage from the Italian Alps and the canals of Venice to a community of Italian immigrants in Roseto, Pennsylvania, and then returns the reader to a mountain setting in Big Stone Gap, Virginia, where those seven children were expected to gather around their parents' flower-laden table every evening at 6.

Spend time with the Trigiani sisters and you'll find they're adept at finishing each other's sentences or footnoting their comments. Reading this book is like observing a spirited family gathering. Scattered throughout the book are bits of advice and opinions from the sisters and their mother. Pia stresses the importance of making friends with the local butcher. Toni advocates the use of only dark meat chicken to accompany her Grandmom

Adriana Trigiani in mid-story, as sister Toni waits to sign books. *Photo by Fred Sauceman.*

Trigiani's polenta. Mary says, "I swear that I did not know we were Italian until we moved to Virginia."

The sisters recall their first encounter with spaghetti as it was served at Big Stone Gap Elementary School. "We were all excited because they said we were having spaghetti," remembers Adriana. "So this meant we were going to have 'eye-talian,' which we were very thrilled about. So we go into the cafeteria and the noodles were very short. That was the first thing. They were shaped like spaghetti, but they were so boiled. *Al dente* was not in the lexicon. You could see through them, and you could probably mash them into a clump in your hand, which we were not used to. And they were rinsed, which we never do. On top of them was basically chili. It had nothing to do with spaghetti as we know it."

The Trigianis never rinsed the noodles, Adriana says, because doing so removes the flavor and reduces their capacity to hold sauce.

"Autumn was my favorite time in Big Stone Gap, always," she told me. "People used to still be able to burn their leaves in the 1970s, and there was that smell. I'd hang out up on the hill with my best friend as the sun would go down. We could talk for hours. Then I would walk home and the first thing I would see would be my mother in the kitchen window with the strainer and the steam coming up, and she would disappear behind the steam. And then you'd know you were having spaghetti, which was my favorite night."

There's an element in all the recipes in *Cooking with My Sisters* that comes through as brightly as the chopped basil leaves in the stuffed and rolled steak dish called *braciole*, as cleanly as the fresh lemon juice in the sauce of garlic and oil for capellini pasta, and as boldly as the pink-rimmed pickled eggs. That element is respect. Respect for the traditions of Italy, for the pound cake and beans-and-cornbread cuisine of Appalachia, and respect for the blessings of family.

Some of the recipes in the book came from an unexpected source, hidden from even the closest of relatives, in the kitchen of the Trigiani sisters' paternal grandmother, Yolanda "Viola" Trigiani.

"After she died, we were cleaning out that kitchen," writes Adriana in the foreword. "The oven broke and needed repairs. When my husband pulled it out of the wall, a flurry of small papers flew out from underneath. Caught between the bottom of the oven and the overstuffed drawer just under it were little scraps of paper that floated around like confetti. These scraps bore Grandmom's familiar script. At first, I wondered if Grandmom had been a secret poet like Emily Dickinson, or whether she had stashed love letters from a handsome suitor. No, she had tucked away something of even greater importance: recipes."

The Trigianis are as quick with a laugh as they are with the sauté pan. In the book Adriana recounts her mother's horror when the children learned, in Southwest Virginia, the very Southern practice of pouring peanuts into Coca-Cola.

Adriana tells me the story of her devoutly Roman Catholic father's visit to the assistant principal of the school in Big Stone Gap, Virginia, and how he complained about his children being served hamburgers on Fridays during Lent. "Don't worry," the school official responded. "There's no meat in those hamburgers. They're all soy."

The Trigiani family had resettled in Big Stone Gap so Anthony could open a blouse factory, providing jobs and a future for hundreds of people in this coal-mining community.

Included in *Cooking with My Sisters* is a 200-year-old Italian recipe for buttermilk cake, which was in great demand for social events in Big Stone Gap.

"When the buttermilk cake hit Big Stone Gap, that was pretty profound," says Adriana. "The women in Big Stone Gap make cakes like the best bakers in the world. Their pound cakes are phenomenal, and that buttermilk cake fit right in. It's a great church supper cake because it's like the loaves and fishes. The thing's huge, and it never goes away."

Anthony Trigiani loved to visit the music store at the Fort Henry Mall in Kingsport, Tennessee, where he'd play the piano for hours. He loved to take in old-time musical performances while sitting on the mismatched carpet swatches at the Carter Fold in Maces Spring, Virginia, where he taught his guests the history of clogging. And he took his own turn at the stove in the family's Victorian home in Big Stone Gap, where he created his steak and onion dish, as prized an inheritance as the Trigiani sisters could ever share.

Anthony Trigiani's Steak and Onions

2 large sweet onions, diced
6 garlic cloves, peeled and thinly sliced
1/4 pound bacon strips, diced (or pancetta if available)
6 tablespoons olive oil
1 28-ounce can tomato purée
2 cups beef stock
1 pound beef steaks (preferably chuck, thinly sliced)
2 cups fresh white mushrooms, thinly sliced
1 28-ounce can artichoke hearts, rinsed, drained, and cut into chunks
2 cups red wine
Salt and freshly ground black pepper to taste

In a heavy, deep skillet, sauté the onions, garlic, and bacon in the olive oil until translucent. Lower the heat and add the tomato purée thinned with the beef stock. Stir the mixture and let it simmer. Then add the steaks to the skillet and cook over low heat. Add the mushrooms, artichokes, and red wine. Season with salt and pepper. Lower the heat and cook covered for twenty minutes or until the steaks are tender. Roasted potatoes make an excellent accompaniment. Serves four.

Grandma Accetturo's Tortellini

Sorrento's Bistro, Banner Elk, North Carolina

The more a restaurant owner invokes the memory of his grandmother, the better the food. It's a basic rule of dining out. Antonette Accetturo never made it to the mountains of North Carolina. She never crossed the Atlantic to America. She never even left her native Sicily, but her spirit guides her grandson's restaurant in Banner Elk, North Carolina.

Sorrento's Bistro is solidly and proudly Italian. Owner Angelo Accetturo and his family have created, in ski resort country, a place as true to Italian tradition as any big-city trattoria. Sorrento's wouldn't be out of place on a side street in Palermo.

Just inside the front door sits a 20-pound hunk of prosciutto from Parma, Italy. Cut silica-thin, it's served on an appetizer plate with chunks of flaking Parmesano-Reggiano cheese, strips of roasted red peppers, and bright-green basil leaves.

Angelo explains how his Sicilian grandmother saved every scrap of ham, even the part she called the heel. The Tortellini Sorrento is Mrs. Accetturo's recipe. The pasta is served in what the staff calls a "pink sauce," primarily cream, colored with tomato and seasoned with prosciutto and sautéed onions.

The marinara sauce is a Sicilian heirloom recipe, too. "Start with good tomatoes," Angelo implores. "Garlic, good tomatoes, basil, a touch of salt and pepper, and first-press olive oil make a light sauce. This is not the kind of sauce you cook all day. Forty-five minutes and it's done. And that includes the time you spent peeling the garlic."

Sit at Sorrento's bar and you're treated not to goldfish crackers, pretzels, or salted nuts but rather to martini glasses full of marinated green and black olives. Manager Geri Palazzo says the idea came from a Philadelphia bar. The olives there were served plain, she remembers. The Accetturo family added the Italian-style marinade. Olive oil and garlic are two of the six ingredients, but the exact recipe is a secret.

Geri Palazzo, Sorrento's Bistro, Banner Elk, North Carolina. *Photo by Murray Lee, MurrayLee.com.*

Exhausted from selling feather boas and incense, the proprietor of Expressions, "the number one alternative store in North Carolina" next door, comes over for a White Pie. The pizza is topped with ricotta, mozzarella, Parmesan, and Romano cheeses.

The Accetturos converted a wine cellar into a locals room, with an imported Italian slate floor, high-back leather chairs, velvet curtains, Mediterranean arches, and columns. Despite such stylish surroundings, even drippy skiers just down from Sugar Mountain are welcome.

Sorrento's is located in a corner among Banner Elk's Village Shops. Just follow the arias of the Italian tenor over the loudspeakers and keep walking as the smell of sizzling garlic intensifies.

In the same complex, Angelo runs a neighborhood bar called the 19th Hole, where red neon lips hang just opposite the restroom doors.

Sorrento's World Famous Bistro
Village Shops
Banner Elk, North Carolina
(828) 898-5214

Corvina, Corvina—
Ricardo's Argentine Fish

The Lomo Grill, Waynesville, North Carolina

Western North Carolinians made down payments on Buicks at 44 Church Street in Waynesville nine years before the stock market crash dented car-buying habits. A later generation toted in shirts for starching and pants for pressing at Central Cleaners in that same building. Today, between old brick walls and under the original tin ceiling, Argentinean and Italian cooking styles converge with Appalachian gardening techniques at the Lomo Grill.

Ricardo and Suzanne Fernandez have transformed the boxy building into a Mediterranean indoor patio—a reflection, they say, of all the places they've lived. Ricardo came north from Buenos Aires, Suzanne south from Boston, to celebrate food in this Appalachian town where pickups and Jaguars compete for on-street parking space.

New-wave, new-age art galleries alternate with decades-old dispensaries of life's basics on Main Street in Waynesville. You can buy coffee in a Styrofoam cup or a foaming flavored cappuccino. The Mast General Store does a steady trade selling farmers' overalls, while across the street artisans advertise rocks that have been collected from the surrounding mountains, drilled, and fitted with wicks and oil receptacles to illuminate that special corner of the home.

Waynesville is a town that embraces twenty-first-century tourist development tricks and yet preserves its mountain soul. It's a town that still supports a newsstand, the Open Air Market, where stone weights protect the *Charlotte Observer* and even the *Miami Herald* from mountain winds as readers flip through shelves of paperbacks, sip grape drinks, and eat hot roasted peanuts at 35 cents for 3 ounces.

Suzanne labels it "an authentic, walkable downtown that doesn't fold up when the tourists go home." At the Lomo, the Fernandez family takes care of the locals as graciously as any of the diners who navigate congested inter-

The Lomo Grill. *Photo courtesy Deborah Benson Cantwell.*

states from Atlanta, Georgia, for one of the South's few Argentinean dining experiences.

Ricardo says Argentines eat more beef per capita than any other nation in the world, and he is a master at preparing it. All the beef served at the Lomo, named after the Argentinean word for tenderloin, is from grass-fed cattle and free of both steroids and growth hormones. Flown in from Australia, the meat is lean, strong in taste, and rich in color. Ricardo's only seasonings are coarse salt and the flames of North Carolina applewood.

Dressed completely in black like the rest of the Lomo staff, Ricardo tends the fire in full view of diners. Shortly after a cut of beef is served, he glances toward the table inquisitively. Diners and chef trade raised thumbs and smiles.

No additional seasoning is needed at the table, either, but true to Argentinean tradition, Ricardo provides a ramekin of *chimichurri*, an oily, herby, garlicky blend of bold flavors good for dipping slices of beef, chunks of Paesano bread, or fingers.

His other Latin condiment, Mucho Macho Sauce, is an orange-red purée of twenty different peppers. Eaten by itself, it is stunningly hot. Taken in combination with other dishes, such as fruit or cheese, it is less likely to vault you up for a close inspection of the design work on the tin ceiling. Yellow Branch Farm, over in Robbinsville, spikes one of its farmstead cheeses with what Suzanne calls her husband's "magic potion."

Corvina, a saltwater whitefish, is flown in regularly from the waters off the Argentinean coast. Like the beef, it needs little in the way of ornamentation—only lemon, salt, and the good timing of Ricardo's kitchen staff. He describes the flavor of the nearly two-inch-thick filets as "a cross between grouper and snapper."

The Lomo menu is heavily dominated by Italian dishes, from pizza baked in a brick oven, a Monday evening feature, to Cannelloni della Mamma, the original recipe of Ricardo's Italian mother, the late Edith Battini. Thin crepes bulge with chicken, Mamma Battini's red and white sauces, and cheese.

"The largest population of Italians outside Italy is found in Argentina," Ricardo says. "Our food and language are influenced by Italians." Suzanne says that fact is reflected in her husband's daily question, around 9 o'clock each morning, "What are we having for lunch?"

These two former urbanites have adapted to the rhythms of the mountains, and their menu shows it. They buy organic foods from local producers and small farmers and grow much of what is served on their tables themselves—herbs, garlic, asparagus, berries, lettuce, and tomatoes.

"Nothing takes the place of picking your own and bringing it here," Suzanne says. "Diners unaccustomed to the taste of fresh spinach often ask us what else is in it, and they are amazed when we tell them only olive oil and garlic."

The crowning touch to a meal at the Lomo is an Argentinean dessert called Panqueque de Banana. Mamma Battini's crepes reappear, this time rolled around banana slices spread with *dulce de leche*, a thick, rich, brown sauce made by caramelizing sugar in milk. More sugar is sprinkled on top and browned with a blowtorch, and the crepe is served with ice cream, whipped cream, or both and a sprig of mint from the garden. It's a sweet, hot, cold, sticky, soft, crunchy, and colorful dessert that brings South America to the Southern Highlands.

The Lomo Grill
44 Church Street
Waynesville, North Carolina
(828) 452-5222

There's Never Been a Speck of Ham in the Place—A Remembrance of Harold's

Harold's Kosher-Style Food Center, Knoxville, Tennessee

Addie and Harold Shersky worked behind this counter in Knoxville, Tennessee, for over fifty years. *Photo by Fred Sauceman.*

South Gay Street in Knoxville, Tennessee, was a bustling Jewish business district in the middle of the twentieth century. Fifty years later, Harold's Kosher-Style Food Center was the only reminder of that remarkable period in the history of East Tennessee's largest city. Harold's survived amid pawn shops and rescue missions, encircled by the smell of roasting coffee from the JFG plant up the street. Robert Shersky was the city's kosher butcher in the

1940s. His son Harold and Harold's wife Addie celebrated fifty-five years in the delicatessen business on September 1, 2003.

When Harold and Addie first started serving the best smoked tongue sandwich south of the Lower East Side of Manhattan, there were 766 Jews in Knox County out of some 220,000 citizens. One of them was jeweler Max Friedman, who served on the Knoxville City Council for two decades. I can imagine Max putting down his hot pastrami sandwich on the counter at Harold's and, in mid-bite, offering a fellow diner some political advice with his familiar preface, "I'll be frank with you."

The highway to Knoxville's McGee-Tyson Airport is named in memory of Max Friedman, but his jewelry store downtown is now a law office. As the building was deteriorating in the 1980s, I remember looking at it from the TVA towers, noticing that two letters had dropped off the sign and thinking, "There are newcomers here in town who probably think *Ma Fredman* was a real person."

The population of Knoxville shifted west, and the Jewish businesses along Gay and Vine all closed down—except for Harold's.

For over half a century, Harold and Addie labored behind that counter, beginning in the early hours of the morning when they dished up one of the finest breakfasts around: scrambled eggs with lox and onions, a slice of tomato on the side, and a heavily buttered, toasted bagel. Three times a week they made Harold's Lithuanian mother Dora's matzo ball soup. Sometimes the matzo balls sank to the bottom of the bowl, as Harold's sister liked them, and sometimes they floated among the carrots, onion, and celery.

In October of 2003, I gave a talk at the University of Mississippi about the foodways of my native Southern Appalachia. For the attendees at the sixth annual Southern Foodways Symposium I shared my "Mountain Diner's Diary," which included a photograph of Harold and Addie Shersky behind that old and familiar counter on Gay Street. I related their story. I remarked about how Harold had told me once that there'd never been a speck of ham in the place. I bragged on the potato knishes and latkes. I talked about Harold and Addie's devotion to each other and their perseverance, how they kept their Jewish heritage alive through the gift of food. I described how their personalities naturally brought people together.

On Harold and Addie's fiftieth wedding anniversary, some friends gave them a plaque with the inscription "Catholics United for Kosher Food."

When I returned to my office at East Tennessee State University the next week, one of life's strange and inexplicable coincidences happened. I began catching up on my stack of newspapers. In the October 3 issue of the *Knoxville News-Sentinel,* on the very day of my talk, there was a story about the death of Addie Shersky. She had departed this world the night before.

In the spring of 2005, at age eighty-six, Harold turned over the day-to-day management of the Knoxville landmark to a friend, with a blessing and a requirement—that the menu stay true to the Addie days. Sadly, though, Harold's closed a few weeks later.

Harold's Kosher-Style Food Center was formerly located at 131 South Gay Street, Knoxville, Tennessee. For further information on Knoxville's Jewish history, see *A Separate Circle: Jewish Life in Knoxville, Tennessee* by Wendy Lowe Besmann (University of Tennessee Press, 2001).

A Curry of Mountain Buttermilk from Madonna's Swimming Coach

Gage's Towne House, Nickelsville, Virginia

Judy Gilmer and Nazim Hack garnish chicken curry. *Photo by Larry Smith.*

Chicken curry and country biscuits are rarely partnered on restaurant menus. But at Gage's Towne House in Nickelsville, Virginia, these two disparate dishes share a common ingredient in the kitchen of Nazim Hack: buttermilk. Southern biscuits rely on buttermilk for texture and flavor, but to find it in chicken curry is offbeat, odd.

Curries usually depend on either yogurt or coconut milk for thickening and as balancing agents for spices. Nazim, who was born and raised in the Caribbean, was accustomed to blending in coconut milk, but in Nickelsville that commodity is as rare as rendered lard in New York City. Falling back on his own resources and taking advantage of what was available at the store across the street, he experimented with buttermilk and loved the results. His country curry includes broccoli and mushrooms and is served over long-grain basmati rice.

Drawing on childhood memories of island feasts, Nazim makes his own yellow hot sauce to drizzle on top of the curry. He brings the sauce to the table cold for a pleasing contrast to the steaminess of the curry. Connections in New York City send him Jamaican yellow peppers, which he cures with lemon to make the tropical condiment.

Nazim's New York ties run deep. He once worked for Donald Trump as a swimming instructor at his International Hotel and Spa, with Madonna as one of his pupils. Taken as he was with the pop diva, it was Judy Gilmer from Scott County, Virginia, who really caught his attention. After ten swimming lessons and a salty margarita, they became engaged. Judy had worked for the Swiss Army company and was directed to learn to swim by her doctor.

After a brief career as "weather girl" for Knoxville's WBIR television, the former Gate City High School beauty queen had made her way to New York to pursue a career in modeling. She acted in a few television movies, posed for several magazine covers, and even recorded an album, but at 5 feet 4 inches she always felt she was about two inches too short to move to the next level in her career. She and Nazim left the city to take up permanent residence near her girlhood home in the mountains of Southwest Virginia and raise a family, which soon grew to four children. Gage's is named for their eldest son.

Nazim swam in the 1975 Pan-American Games and the 1976 Olympics in Montreal for Guyana. He now shares his knowledge as assistant coach of the state champion swimming team at Dobyns-Bennett High School in Kingsport, Tennessee.

Gage's menu is a reflection of the complicated cultural influences that have shaped the life of Nazim Hack. There's Asian style fried rice, seasoned with American country ham, alongside chicken egg rolls and shrimp tacos. Nazim's philosophy is: "If you want a dish, we cook it for you." That may mean killed lettuce with Scott County garden produce or Jamaican rice and beans.

Gage's Towne House
Highway 71
Nickelsville, Virginia
(276) 479-1900

Virginia Würste

Gasthaus Edelweiss, Weber City, Virginia

As he was preparing to take her to America for the first time as his bride in 1954, Edwin Carter made no grandiose promises to sixteen-year-old Ingrid Pfeiffer.

"Lots of GIs told German girls all kinds of stories," remembers Ingrid. "But he was quiet. I had no illusions. When I got to America, though, it was like going to Disney World."

Edwin never promised Ingrid he'd build her a restaurant from the ground up, with his own hands, but one day he would do just that. There wasn't much talk about dining out in war-torn, battle-tired Berlin during the Carters' courtship on the western side of the divided city.

What Ingrid and Edwin did talk about, though, was getting by—how Germans saved every potato peeling, how they traded linens that had survived the bombings for those potatoes.

They didn't talk cooking, because Ingrid didn't know how to do much more than boil the water they had to lug home from the street corner where horses used to drink, since the bombed-out pipes still hadn't been repaired. But she had watched her mother Charlotte season and marinate *Sauerbraten*. She had taken mental notes as her mother chopped eggs and diced tomatoes for her own amalgamated version of German potato salad.

"Mother could make miracles out of nothing. After the war, that's what you had to do."

Ingrid knew there'd come a time when she'd want to recreate the sweets and sours of her mother's kitchen. Gradually, with practice on pots of red cabbage and platters of potato dumplings, it all came back. On May 13, 1987, the Carters put out the *Wilkommen* sign in front of their very own German restaurant, Gasthaus Edelweiss, near the railroad tracks in the Southwest Virginia mountain burg of Weber City.

Edwin and Ingrid Carter. *Photo by Fred Sauceman.*

"We chose to call it a guest house because we wanted a cozy, homey feel, and Edelweiss because everybody knows the song from *The Sound of Music*," says Ingrid.

Between shifts in the lab at Eastman Chemical Company across the Tennessee line in Kingsport, Edwin built the pitched-roof, cottage-style restaurant by himself. He built it right next to their home after their youngest son graduated from high school, when, as Ingrid puts it, "We needed a new baby."

Ingrid has developed the recipes, and it is she who greets guests three days a week while Edwin cuts pork tenderloin and transforms it into schnitzels of several varieties.

For classic German dishes like *Jägerschnitzel*, the mushroom-topped, brown-sauced "hunter's cutlet," Edwin prefers American pork over veal.

"They use veal in Europe, but here they don't know how to cut it, and they beat it to death. It's costly and you lose half. You get a certain flavor out of the meat by the way you cut it. We cut our pork tenderloin with the grain, dip it in eggs and breading, and lay it on the grill with butter at not too high a heat. It cooks all the way through and browns evenly instead of in spots."

Catch Gasthaus Edelweiss on the right day and you can surround the schnitzel with a pile of Ingrid's incomparable parsley-sprinkled short noodles called *Spätzle.*

For his kitchen work Edwin sports a white-and-red Schaller & Weber apron, a confident advertisement that the Carters' sausages are shipped in from this highly reputable, family-owned New York City business that has been satisfying Americans' desire for wurst since 1937.

Gasthaus Edelweiss offers all-pork bratwurst, *Bauernwurst* of beef and pork, an Edwin Carter-approved veal sausage called *Weisswurst,* all-beef *Knackwurst,* and long, thin *Wienerwürstchen* that Ingrid says children enjoy. All these are served with imported German mustard. "Currywurst" can be any two sausages covered in a thick, spiced purée of tomatoes, onions, and peppers—Edwin's take on a sauce Ingrid recollects from her girlhood in Berlin.

Cabbage comes in two forms at Gasthaus Edelweiss: as thinly shredded, wine-soaked sauerkraut, listed on the menu as *Weinkraut,* and as the sweet and sour, deep-purply-red *Rotkohl* cabbage dish, a special request we sent in when Ingrid catered our wedding rehearsal dinner in the late summer of 1980.

Germans' and Appalachians' mutual love of potatoes helped Ingrid make the transition from Berlin to Scott County, and there are potatoes on her restaurant table every day. The Berliner potato salad is cold and prepared with cream, while the Bavarian is warm and made with vinegar, oil, and bacon.

Ingrid does all the baking—usually three or four Central European desserts each day. Her *Bienenstisch* is a two-layer cake filled with Bavarian cream and topped with buttered and sugared almonds. The name literally means "bee sting," and Ingrid says if you eat a piece outside, you'll quickly find out why. She makes streusel with plums, streusel with apples, chocolatey

Orange Crème Torte, Mocha Rum Torte, and, a dessert she says every German knows how to make, an *Obsttorte* or fruit tart. It consists of one layer of cake baked in a flan pan, topped with fresh fruit, and glazed.

When Edwin brought Ingrid to Appalachia, she knew almost no English and picked up the language first by reading comic books and associating the pictures with the words, oftentimes under the hair dryer at a Gate City, Virginia, beauty shop. It was her long hair that first caught Edwin's eye on a Berlin street. Ingrid's hair was so lengthy that the beauty shop appointments were two-hour affairs, affording her plenty of time for absorbing American and mountain idioms.

The parents of five children, Edwin and Ingrid revisit her homeland often, now with their grandchildren. Germany is never far away from her thinking. It's there in her plates of *Rouladen*, sirloin sliced thin, filled with pickles, seasoning, and mustard, rolled, browned in butter, and sauced. It's there in the shards of the Berlin wall in a glass case below the fiftieth anniversary wedding vase the local German club gave them.

Ingrid thinks often of her mother's sacrifices in the days after World War II and the death of her father Hans, a professional bookbinder, probably somewhere in Poland, where his last letter to his family was postmarked. After the adversity, suffering, and deprivation she'd lived through, Ingrid opened Gasthaus Edelweiss as a way to bring delight into her adopted mountain home. There she honors the proud culinary traditions of the place she left behind as a new bride half a century ago.

Gasthaus Edelweiss
137 South Dogwood Drive
Weber City, Virginia
(276) 386-3724

A Campeche Kitchen Recreated

The children of Romeo and Candelaria Jimenez rush home from Woodland Elementary School in Johnson City, Tennessee, for an after-school snack—not potato chips or Pop Tarts but rather *posole*, a spicy pork and hominy stew their mother learned to make back home in the state of Campeche on Mexico's Yucatan Peninsula.

Romeo, Jr., Hector, and Kelamy Jimenez watch *SpongeBob SquarePants* faithfully and can easily navigate the show's internet Anchovy Feeding Frenzy Game. They've been microwaving popcorn ever since they grew tall enough to reach the oven. Kelamy makes a game of pointing out what groceries go in the refrigerator. They warmly welcome visitors, give them a tour of their roomy new home, and practice their English. They pour glasses of fruit punch. These personable and energetic children absorb and enjoy American popular culture.

The lives of the Jimenez family represent a vigorous blend of Mexican and American tastes. On the refrigerator door are three things: an image of the Virgin Mary with text that reads, *Madre Santisima, sana nuestras heridas*—"Holiest Mother of God, heal our wounds"; Disney's Lilo and Stitch; and a $1 coupon for the next joint purchase of Doritos and Mountain Dew.

At mealtime the family's memories of their Mexican origins are strongest. While her husband is finishing up his latest construction project, Candelaria ends her day of cleaning houses around town with a trip to the grocery store, where she carefully selects the leanest London broil, the lightest-feeling green cabbage, and the brightest orange habanero peppers for the evening meal. Despite a physically demanding full-time job cleaning six homes a week, she cooks a complete dinner almost every night for her family.

During our shopping trip, Candelaria points out her favorite Hispanic products. Sazón Goya is a powder of dried cilantro and achiote used to flavor and color rice. A Nestlé product, Media Crema, is mixed with commercial sour cream to make a topping for flautas, tortillas that are stuffed, rolled into the shape of flutes, and fried. Valentina brand Salsa Picante, described as "extra hot with chiles and spices," is available all over the region. In the Jimenez household, it revs up bowls of popcorn. A preferred drink of the Jimenez children is hot chocolate, made with milk and wedges of Abuelita ("little grandmother"), a rich chocolate flavored with cinnamon, also produced by Nestlé.

Once the groceries are in their proper place at home, Candelaria's niece Onoria Diaz takes charge of tortillas. In a special lavender-colored bowl she blends Maseca Corn Masa with American bread flour and some water. When the dough is smooth, she breaks off pieces, rolls them in her hands, and sticks the flat discs around the outside of the bowl. All turn out almost exactly the same size. She lines a tortilla press with rounds of wax paper and patiently transforms each circle of dough into a thin tortilla.

Sitting across two eyes of the General Electric stove is a *comal*, a long, oval-shaped cast-iron griddle with handles, similar to the fish fryers found in area antique stores. Onoria lightly oils the vessel and fries three tortillas at a time, turning them once with her unprotected fingers. When they inflate like balloons, she removes them to a basket lined with a towel. The finished stack reaches about 4 inches high.

Making tortillas is an everyday job in this household. Leftovers are fried in oil, broken into pieces, and lightly salted for snacks the next day.

Candelaria meticulously slices the London broil, a 3-pound cut of top round, as thinly as her knife and fingers will allow. The blade glides down the entire length of the slab of meat, parallel to the countertop, and by the time she's through her platter is piled with beef.

Just as her Mayan ancestors did ages before food processors and blenders, with a pestle she grinds together fresh cloves of garlic, whole black peppercorns, whole cumin seeds, and salt. She's adept in making sure nothing jumps out of the small bowl, not even the hard, round peppercorns. To the paste she adds freshly squeezed lime juice and works the mixture into the meat with her fingers. She stops only long enough to acknowledge an egg-laden wasp's nest her daughter has collected and placed in a plastic bag for science class.

Candelaria Jimenez teaches her daughter Kelamy the art of the tortilla. *Photo by Fred Sauceman.*

As Candelaria proceeds with the remainder of the dinner, she fries the steak, a handful at a time, in a 10-inch skillet while black beans seasoned with home-rendered lard simmer nearby. The freezer is packed with unwrapped pork and none of it, not even the fat, is wasted. Occasionally, as preparation progresses, Candelaria mashes, stirs, and seasons the beans with salt straight out of the cardboard container.

While steak sizzles and beans boil, the family pauses to catch *CNN en Español*'s coverage of the "Guerra en Irak" as American troops greet their families in Spanish.

Two different salsas are on the menu for tonight, one cooked and one uncooked. For the first, tomatoes and jalapeño peppers are boiled, puréed, and salted. The uncooked salsa is more piquant. Holding the stems and avoiding contact with the flesh of the peppers, Onoria deftly dices habaneros with the skill and speed of a culinary school graduate. She makes quick work of a red onion, too, and minces fresh cilantro, stems and all. Salt and the ever-present lime juice complete the combination. She lightly dips her finger into the finished product and touches her tongue carefully. The balance of hot and sour is perfect.

Candelaria finds a free eye on the stove, heats up some oil, and fries a panful of long-grain rice from the local Sav-A-Lot. Water, salt, red onion, and a tomato she has sliced in textbook fashion without a cutting board complete the ingredients, which simmer beneath a dinner plate for twenty minutes.

She cuts a head of curly leaf cabbage in half, shreds it by hand, sprinkles on even more lime juice and salt, and in seconds the dish called *repollo picado* is complete, no cooking required.

A feast evocative of the tables of Campeche is served. Neighbors come over to fill their plates with meat, beans, and rice. Both salsas and the cabbage are sprinkled on top. Diners then paint the insides of their corn tortillas with beans, add a few spoons of rice, toss in steak strips, and dress their tacos with more salsa and tart cabbage strips.

The women who prepared the meal stay in the kitchen to begin the cleanup while the men eat, quietly but gratefully. Hands reach for the tortilla basket often and both salsa bowls are emptied, the hotter one first.

The Jimenez family has observed area grocery stores carrying more and more Hispanic products since they came to Johnson City in 1998. In addition to the small, locally owned markets scattered around the region, they can find most of what they need at more "mainstream" stores such as Food City and Wal-Mart.

Every day this hard-working Mexican immigrant family recreates Mesoamerican flavors amid the mountains of East Tennessee. They miss sunny Campeche and have yet to develop an appreciation for mountain snowfalls, but they're carving out a living, a rich life, and an education for their three children through hard work and frugality—lessons learned and refined on both sides of the border.

3

Waterfront Fare

We see diners turn into divers
and get magnetized by Iron Mountain.

Northeast Tennessee Boat Dock Dining

The Captain's Table, Sonny's Marina, and Lakeview

"There's nothing like this in Iowa," concluded one of the Midwesterners as the sun set outside the dining room window of the Captain's Table Restaurant at Lakeshore Resort.

Conversation often ceases among otherwise talkative guests, who are drawn to the view of tree-lined Watauga Lake near the Northeast Tennessee community of Hampton. At a window-side table you're 300 feet above the lakeshore on a steep, wooded bank. Iron Mountain rises up about a mile across the water.

Hand-holding couples amble along an old-fashioned boardwalk, their quiet concentration occasionally broken by a boat motor or a dance tune emanating from the bottom floor of the restaurant as the Hampton Elementary School prom heats up.

Owner Kathy Taylor keeps the restaurant going upstairs without interruption, since the popular food choice among the prom crowd is quick and simple: chicken fingers. Kathy and her parents, Ted and Betty Tipton, have operated this family business on Highway 321 for well over forty years. They rent out motel rooms and cabins, pontoons and speedboats, sell fishing licenses, moor watercraft, sauté sea scallops, charbroil filet mignon, and fry dill pickles dressed with tartar sauce and salsa.

Theirs is an ambitious menu, offered from spring until autumn on the shores of one of the cleanest lakes in America. The 6,430-acre body of water was completed in 1948 by the Tennessee Valley Authority. Two thousand feet above sea level, it is the highest reservoir in the Tennessee River System.

In addition to the fish nets, shells, and sand dollars, the restaurant displays a collection of old outboard motors. On the extensive menu is a salad dressing so good it could serve double duty as a beverage. It's a combination of bold Asian flavors—hoisin sauce, ginger, rice vinegar, sesame oil, soy, garlic, and red pepper flakes.

Lora Harris, the Captain's Table. *Photo by Fred Sauceman.*

Kathy's Greek linguini is layered with fresh tomatoes, mushrooms, black olives, onions, and feta cheese and completed with shrimp, scallops, or both. Her Oyster Crisp combines fresh oysters with bacon, Swiss cheese, and

Sonny's Runabout Café is a float-through restaurant. *Photo by Fred Sauceman.*

cream, finished with coarse bread crumbs and baked until the oysters are just at the point of doneness.

At Sonny's Marina on Boone Lake near Johnson City, Tennessee, oysters undergo similar transformations. Owner Mickii Carter got her ideas from a visit to the kitchen at a restaurant in Apalachicola, Florida, one of the nation's most prolific oyster-producing regions. Her Oysters Regal consists of fresh oysters on the half shell, topped with two cheeses and jalapeño peppers, baked, and then crisped briefly under a broiler.

Many of the dishes at Sonny's come straight out of Mickii's kitchen, including her chicken quesadillas with black beans, corn, and tomatoes. She makes the key lime pie and turtle cheesecake herself.

Eating at Sonny's is like having a party on your neighbor's backyard deck. You hear the smack of flip-flops on the dock, feel a light wind off of

Lakeview's massive fried grouper sandwich. *Photo by Fred Sauceman.*

Boone Lake, and catch the smell of grill-marked Black Angus hamburgers. The dining area is covered, but it extends out into the lake since it was constructed in 1953, prior to the Tennessee Valley Authority's building restrictions.

"It's the sunshine and the water," says Mickii, a former mayor of Johnson City who had no previous experience in managing restaurants or marinas. "This place has a real beach feel to it, and we say in our advertising that you've never been so close to a getaway."

Mallard ducks make frequent water landings using their webbed feet like skis. Huge, dark carp create commotion when parents bring their children down to the water to share with the wildlife the remnants of an uneaten burger bun.

Customers call in burger orders from cell phones while riding pontoons across the lake, and float-through diners who arrive by boat at the Runabout Café are treated to free in-water parking. For those who need a tune-up, Sonny's employs two full-time mechanics.

The Captain's Table Restaurant at Lakeshore Resort
2285 Highway 321
Hampton, Tennessee
(423) 725-2201

A tune-up of a different sort is available bar-side. Thirteen different beers are offered on tap, but when the Cothran family owned the place in the 1950s and 1960s, ordering beer had to be done covertly. The code words for beer were "baloney sandwich." An out-of-towner came to the dock and ordered one, unaware of the system. He was puzzled when he opened the brown paper bag and discovered a cold can of Budweiser.

Near the Tri-City Regional Airport, where the Holston and Watauga rivers converge to form Boone Lake, sits Lakeview Marina and the Marker 2 Grille. The marina boasts the largest indoor boat storage in the Tri-Cities.

Owners Patty and Ken Parrish are transplanted North Carolinians. Patty says she prepared for a career in the food industry through motherhood, and her education as a nurse has come in handy in the marina business. She has repaired feet cut by boat propellers and re-hydrated sunstroke victims.

Customers' photographs are packed under the glass table coverings indoors, and the neighbor's lumbering black Labrador naps outside. To the Parrishes, this business is home.

To create Jeff's Famous Burger their son embellishes a traditional cheeseburger with barbecue sauce, bacon, and a fried onion ring. The fried grouper sandwich approaches foot-long status and is nearly 2 inches thick.

Sonny's Marina and Runabout Café
109 One Street
Gray, Tennessee
(423) 283-4014

Ken's experience as a salesman for Dillard Paper taught him the importance of cross-training employees. The staff at Lakeview can sell you a koozie, wash your boat, pump your gas, and teach novice boat owners how to navigate their craft.

Whether you order black olives stuffed with Asiago cheese at the Captain's Table, homemade potato chips at Sonny's Marina, or cinnamon-sugared sweet potato fries at Lakeview, dining dockside is summertime delight on the lakes of Northeast Tennessee.

Lakeview Marina
474 Lakeside Dock Drive
Kingsport, Tennessee
(423) 323-1054

A Holston River Rescue

Riverfront Seafood Company, Kingsport, Tennessee

"Good seafood is not cheap, and cheap seafood is not good." That motto sums up the fish philosophy of Wayne Michelli, owner of the Riverfront Seafood Company Fresh Market and Grill in Kingsport, Tennessee.

Evolving from fish market and live bait shop to one of the region's most varied sources for seafood, Riverfront has established contacts with suppliers throughout the South. These relationships assure customers absolute freshness and a myriad of choices that rival the best coastal seafood houses in America.

All of Riverfront's Gulf shrimp come from the same source in Dulac, Louisiana, and I order them "barbecued." I judge barbecued shrimp by the condition of the napkin after the meal. Mine is a tattered, crumpled, reddened mess. The worse the napkin looks afterward, the better the shrimp.

The barbecue sauce at Riverfront is a cooked-down, thickened mix of chili sauce, oregano, garlic, parsley, hot sauce, lemon juice, plenty of butter, and a special Creole seasoning blended at the restaurant. The sauce colors the shrimp a deep red brown, and to make sure none is wasted, Riverfront provides thick, buttery slabs of toasted French bread for sopping.

Buffalo oysters are among some sixteen appetizers. Gulf bivalves from Bayou La Batre, Alabama, are lightly breaded, cooked until just done, and sauced with a combination of ingredients that normally surround the more common Buffalo chicken wings.

Wayne and Angie Michelli will pick up a recipe or cooking tip just about anywhere. At a restaurant in San Diego, they got the idea to thread bacon squares onto skewers between scallops. They admired Bill Stidham's blackberry cakes he brought to church dinners at the First Assembly of God in Kingsport and talked him out of the recipe. It's turned out to be one of Riverfront's most requested desserts.

Riverfront's daily specials are listed on a chalkboard held by a peculiar, 5-foot crustacean imported from The Philippines.

With the Holston River flowing in the background, Wayne Michelli displays a plate of fresh mahi, tuna, Chilean sea bass, and swordfish. *Photo by Larry Smith.*

In warm weather the lapping of the current against the bank and the swirling of the shoals in the Holston River's South Fork make the deck at Riverfront a scenic and soothing dining spot, at least most of the time.

In July of 2003, David Bowery had just ordered a plate of seafood when he looked up and saw a blond-haired little girl bobbing in the current. She had fallen into the water about 200 yards upstream. Juliann Farmer, then age two, had been riding her red tricycle when she fell off the riverbank and got caught in the current.

David jumped off the deck, hooked his arm around the terrified girl, swam with her to the bank, and handed her off to paramedic Gary Collins, who just happened to be eating at the restaurant. He dried her off, wrapped her in blankets, and made sure she was stable and out of danger.

"The only way she's alive today is the grace of God looking over that girl," Wayne Michelli told the *Kingsport Times-News*. "If it had been any other time of day except dinner, or if she had gotten down past the bridge where the rapids are, it would have drowned her."

David Bowery and Juliann's parents, Eric and Brandi Farmer, recounted the story on ABC's *Good Morning America*, but Juliann stayed quiet until the cameras were turned off. Then she said, "I fell in that water. I was riding a tricycle. I saw a snake and a fish and a dolphin."

Brandi says her daughter's tale gets a little bigger every time she tells it.

Riverfront Seafood Company
Fresh Market and Grill
1777 Netherland Inn Road
Kingsport, Tennessee
(423) 245-3474

4

Fancy Digs

We slip cream cake to a Confederate ghost,
target trout from a spring house, mire in sticky toffee pudding,
and bask in the light of home improvement store palm trees.

Undulating Forks and Other Fun Stuff

Savoy, Asheville, North Carolina

Eric Scheffer had been putting off a friend's invitation to Western North Carolina, but the 1994 earthquake epicentered in Northridge, California, near his home in Los Angeles was all the convincing it took for him to head cross-country.

That Thanksgiving he came to see what Asheville was all about, rented a car, and got lost. He ended up on the Blue Ridge Parkway, got out of the car, looked over the leafless November valley, and something hit him. It wasn't a gun barrel, like the one a would-be carjacker pointed at his head back in Southern California that same year. This time the feeling was something he couldn't swat away, couldn't even explain really. He got teary. Geographically disoriented though he was, Eric felt right then and there that the highlands of North Carolina would be his permanent home.

So he said goodbye to a sparkling career, one that had given him unimaginable opportunities: the chance to follow the late comedian George Burns, then ninety-three, as he walked laps around his Olympic-sized Beverly Hills pool, planning the HBO special they would produce together; the chance to turn out rock videos with Cyndi Lauper; the chance to work alongside Oliver Stone on the film *Evita*; the money, the cachet, all left behind for a life as a restaurateur in a mountain town he hardly knew.

All doubts about the move vanished when a tree blew down in the front yard of his new North Asheville home.

"Two guys walked up with a chain saw and asked if they could help me take care of the tree. My Long Island Yankee suspicion immediately kicked in."

The neighbors sliced up the tree, hauled the logs away, cleaned up the sawdust, and wouldn't take a dime.

"Then we sat around and engaged in what they called 'jawin.'"

On a handshake in 2000, Eric bought a Greek diner turned Italian kitchen on Merrimon Avenue in Asheville. He set about creating a "worldly,

Actress and singer Daliah Lavi is a regular at the Savoy, run by former LA film producer Eric Scheffer.
Photo by Fred Sauceman.

contemporary" restaurant where he could engage his passions for people, food, and wine.

He wrote a mission statement and printed it on the back of his menu. Ted Turner, who'd flown in from Atlanta for dinner, complimented him on the language: "…to create an environment where life's most sustaining and essential needs of food and drink are presented with undiminished attention to quality, presentation, and service."

As much as Eric savors a plate of shrimp scampi and a square of tiramisu, he decided to expand beyond Italian. He hired classically French-trained Brian Canipelli as executive chef; Asian-schooled Jimi Ducas as sous chef; and classically Latin-trained Arturo Ruiz as second sous chef. The restaurant's logo is an undulating fork.

Tired of 1980s fusion cuisine and its tendency to force together foods that don't belong, Eric worked with his staff to weave the flavors of France, Asia, Latin America, and Italy. The result he calls "Neocosmopolitan," and he's even trademarked the term.

"It's subtle, not heavy-handed, but it surprises folks," says Eric. "At the same time, we've kept our focus on fresh seafood."

About 6 P.M., six days a week, Brian Canipelli gets a call from Hawaii. It's the Honolulu Fish Company on the line, reporting on the morning's catch and the price per pound. At first light a fleet of the company's six boats, manned by old Japanese fishermen with lines and no nets, floats out to angle for ono, marlin, mahi, sea bass. Eric worked with the Federal Express corporation to create a special package for shipping the fish to Asheville. Within a day of the catch these prizes from Pacific waters are brought to the tables at the Savoy, a restaurant with no storage freezers.

The ono, a meaty, deepwater fish from the barracuda family, is grilled and served alongside a mound of goat cheese grits studded with North Carolina-grown shiitake mushrooms and sauced with a dark, Chianti-mustard demiglaze. Sea bass is pan-seared and plated up with melted leeks, spring peas, fingerling potatoes, prosciutto ham, and caviar cream.

After you unfold your napkin scented with a sprig of fresh herb or even encasing rose petals on special nights, among the first-course choices is a wide bowl of Yukon Gold potato soup. White truffle oil and buttermilk surround seared sea scallops and locally grown oyster mushrooms that absorb the flavors of the soup, whose color almost matches the eighty-four-seat restaurant's mottled yellow walls.

"Savoy is both a destination and a neighborhood restaurant," says Eric. "We're near one of Asheville's older neighborhoods, around Beaver Lake, and we're fortunate to occupy a free-standing building with its own parking lot in a city where parking is tight."

Although Savoy is one of Asheville's most expensive restaurants, Eric says he's never had anyone complain about prices. He's made the Tuscan-style establishment approachable, including the wine list, which features one category entitled "Italian Reds and Other Fun Stuff." Influenced by his wife Heidi, Eric has added several wines from her homeland, Argentina—vintages he describes as "some of the world's best."

Savoy's professional servers take food and wine classes and periodically are given written examinations, assuring they can accurately describe everything from one of Arturo's hot tamales—with chicken, fontina cheese, and salsa verde—to the fifteen greens in a salad.

Eric is accustomed to rubbing shoulders with the famous, so actor Robin Williams's repeat visits don't shake him, nor does an unannounced appearance by Robert Redford. Eric's father Manny was lighting director for *Butterfield 8* and *Splendor in the Grass* and produced the "plop-plop, fizz-fizz" Alka-Seltzer commercials of the 1960s.

Something told me to stage a quick photograph of the stately lady complimenting Eric on the dinner she'd just finished.

"Who was that?" I ask him. "Oh, she was one of the 'Bond girls' in the 1960s. She doesn't live too far from here."

Daliah Lavi, an Israeli beauty who appeared in the movies *Casino Royale* and *Spy with a Cold Nose*, was listed in the September 1963 *Playboy* magazine as one of "Europe's New Sexy Sirens."

Another intriguing lady makes regular appearances at the Savoy. She speaks three languages and plays the piano. She may walk up and ask you what you're eating. She'll tell you about her preferences for steak, asparagus, and garlic mashed potatoes. Jordan is Eric and Heidi's brilliant young daughter, born in 1999 severely premature, weighing less than 1 pound. A big sweet eater, she knows she loves her father's bittersweet chocolate ganache with port-glazed dried cherries, but she's never seen it. Jordan's been blind from birth.

On one level Eric's motto "Regret nothing in life in matters of love and food" describes his approach to Neocosmopolitan cuisine. Once you learn the story of the sightless, spirited little girl who's changed his life, you realize the motto's meaning goes even deeper.

Savoy
641 Merrimon Avenue
Asheville, North Carolina
(828) 253-1077

Appalachian Elegance

Blackberry Farm, Walland, Tennessee

When I ask folks to guess the location of the inn that most consistently tops the Zagat Survey rating the nation's small hotels, most think immediately of New England. Almost no one considers Southern Appalachia. Yet that's where it is, in the tiny Smoky Mountain community of Walland, Tennessee.

Blackberry Farm has quickly earned a reputation as one of America's most elegant country getaways. Escorted to your room by an energetic host who will remember your name for the length of your stay, you're immediately greeted by the notes of a classical composition from a bedside compact disc player. The temptation is to fall instantly into the feather bed and remain there, but you notice a row of white rockers out on the veranda and are drawn to the mountain mists.

Each morning, at your chosen time, a basket of croissants, muffins, and scones and a bowl of fresh, cream-topped berries arrive outside your door. In winter, fires blaze in every building. Guests play backgammon on puffy sofas with pillows crimped like Chinese fortune cookies.

In the gift shop you can purchase a handful of Hurricane Katy flies and a book on trout stream insects to build your confidence while casting for trout in the property's ponds and streams. The best diversion of all in any season is a walk in the woods along the meandering mountain paths. Yet no matter how deep your contemplations, the question "What's for dinner?" will never leave your mind as you anticipate the creations chef John Fleer will place before you in the Main House, creations inspired by the soil, the soul, and the spirit of the Great Smoky Mountains.

A native of nearby North Carolina, John calls his fare "Foothills Cuisine," a blend of rugged and refined, simple and sophisticated.

Visiting his Tidewater Virginia grandparents as a young boy, John helped boil Chesapeake Bay crabs and harvested beans and corn out of the backyard garden. In his kitchen at Blackberry Farm he demonstrates daily his

Chef John Fleer describes a meal of blackberried quail and green tomato aspic at the 2003 Southern Foodways Symposium on the campus of the University of Mississippi. *Photo by Larry Smith.*

reverence for the bounty of the South—its forests, ponds, and garden plots, its basement-lining larders of jams and jellies.

"I refer as often to my great-grandmother's treasured recipe book as I do to my classical training," says John. At the 2003 Southern Foodways Symposium on the University of Mississippi campus, where the theme was Appalachian cooking, he forever altered my opinion of the heretofore-hated aspic of my grandmother's generation by making it out of green tomatoes.

John's parents, both Wake Forest University professors, had hoped he'd make a career of teaching religion at a university, and John graduated from Duke with that intention. But food called and he entered the Culinary Institute of America.

That pedigree armed him with the skills it would take to get the attention of the national food press, but it didn't drive him away from his devotion to the commonplace.

After a dinner of sautéed foie gras, sturgeon caviar sauce, and French lentil ragout, John's talk turns to Muddy Pond Sorghum. He features this Middle Tennessee ingredient in Sunday brunch servings of pear and cider sorghum sorbets with apricot purée. Or he begins a treatise on ramps, the stinky, wild mountain leek he once picked out of a compost pile at the CIA in Hyde Park, New York.

"They weren't nearly as powerful as the ones we forage off the Cherohala Skyway near Tellico Plains, Tennessee, every year," John says. "We have several sources for ramps. Our trout farmer in Robbinsville, North Carolina, forages them for us, we forage ourselves, and we have some folks locally who know our passion for ramps and will deliver when they have extra.

"Many of our guests have never been exposed to this very regional specialty, and they love it. We pickle ramps and use them as a garnish for salads. We freeze the lightly blanched bulbs so they can be served out of season. We make a pesto from the tops, and we make a ramp compound butter."

Like his mountain neighbors he adds ramps to scrambled eggs, but he's also been known to create his own version of green eggs and ham as an *amuse bouche* (amusement for the mouth) with soft scrambled eggs, his house-made ramp pesto, batons of country ham, and fingers of buttered toast.

"A cuisine or an individual cooking style has nothing if it does not have heart and history. For me, Blackberry has become the perfect setting for combining my past experience as a citizen of the South and a traveler of the world with my culinary training. From that union of heart and history, Foothills Cuisine was born."

Well-informed young men and women from the surrounding towns and cities pass trays of John Fleer's creations at Blackberry Farm receptions—small ceramic cups of ham hock consommé with bourbon, spoons of trout caviar, and rectangular sandwiches of foie gras butter and muscadine jelly spread between thin slices of Sally Lunn bread. One server describes these sandwiches as "our take on peanut butter and jelly."

John molds small handfuls of macaroni and cheese and deep-fries them so they can easily be eaten as finger food.

After a plateful of John's Eggs Crockett—two poached eggs with andouille sausage on an angel biscuit with tasso hollandaise—vintner Rob Mondavi of California scoots back from the table and concludes, "I love the South. It's just not the same anywhere else."

John Fleer is always willing to share a recipe or cooking tips. As one wine-warmed guest commented, "Those who know the most, share the most."

Blackberry Farm
1471 West Millers Cove Road
Walland, Tennessee
(800) 557-2203

John Fleer's Blackberry Kir Royale

"The kir is the king of champagne-based aperitifs. This is our own black-berry twist. Passing a tray of these beautiful deep rose-colored flutes is a great way to start a dinner party."

1 bottle dry champagne
1/4 cup blackberry brandy
8 fresh blackberries

Pour the champagne into eight flutes. Add a dash or two of blackberry brandy to each glass and garnish with a blackberry.

From John Fleer, *Blackberry Basics: Recipes from Blackberry Farm* (Walland TN: Blackberry Farm Press, 2002).

Confederate Ghosts in Search of Italian Cream Cake

The Martha Washington Inn, Abingdon, Virginia

Upon entering the parlor of the Martha Washington Inn, if you hear Pete Sheffey wailing, "My pain, my pain," don't bolt for the door or call 911. Pete's just introducing another group of visitors to the ghost of Confederate captain John Stover, who died in the building after being wounded across the street in Plum Alley during the Civil War.

Pete's been telling that story for well over fifty years, and he's logged the longest tenure of any employee at the Abingdon, Virginia, landmark. This great-grandson of slaves got his start feeding chickens and pigs for the Barnhill family in Abingdon. His grandfather Wiley Henry was his entrée to what became a lifelong career and passion—providing comfort, warm hospitality, and detailed history to thousands of guests at the Martha since 1952.

"My grandfather started working here in 1898, before it became an inn," Pete said. "He would escort Martha Washington College students from the train station by horse and buggy. He was a baseball player, a preacher, and a singer, and he remembered meeting folks like Tallulah Bankhead as the Barter Theatre got going. There's a scholarship in his name at Emory and Henry College."

The Martha Washington Inn dates to 1832, when the brick structure was built as a private residence. It later became a finishing school for young ladies, a hospital during the Civil War when the students were forced to learn rudimentary nursing skills, a women's college that attracted pupils from up and down the Eastern Seaboard, and finally an elegant inn. Martha Washington College held its final commencement in 1931, victim to the Great Depression, typhoid epidemics, and declining enrollment.

Captain Stover must have overdone it on hardtack biscuit during the Civil War, because folks say he never shows up in the Dining Room.

"I've never seen the ghost," says Dorothy Boucher, who eats at the inn just about every week during good weather.

Pete Sheffey's been telling ghost stories at "The Martha" for well over half a century. *Photo by Fred Sauceman.*

The inn has been a central part of Dorothy's life. She remembers playing hopscotch right outside the building as a young girl, and her father and his friends strung lights across the back lawn for leisurely games of croquet. One of her great-uncles, William Dyer, served as President of Martha Washington College.

With black vest, bowtie service the Sunday brunch begins with a glass of champagne, a mimosa, or a Bloody Mary. "I always begin with a Bloody Mary, because they have a good bartender here," says Dorothy. "Then I'll have some Southern spoon bread, bacon, a light omelet with cheese, fruit, and a piece of cake."

The Dining Room affords a good balance between casual and fancy. Fresh orchids, daisies, and carnations color each table. Dave Collins moves easily on the piano from "Ring Around the Rosie" to the Notre Dame fight song to "Jeannie with the Light Brown Hair" and a jazzy, tinkly version of the theme from *The Flintstones*.

The Dining Room is called just that, and I appreciate the simplicity. After all, that's how we refer to it in our homes, and that's what the management at the Martha had the good sense to name it.

The Martha Washington is owned by the Camberley corporation. So is the Brown Hotel in downtown Louisville, Kentucky, and there's a tasty connection between the two. The Hot Brown sandwich gets very little play in Tennessee and Virginia, which is odd because it was invented in nearby Kentucky in the 1930s. Roasted turkey is placed on toasted bread and covered with a Mornay sauce, a basic white sauce with cheese. Fried bacon is latticed on top along with sliced tomato. All this is run under a broiler, and the result is one of the world's richest, most satisfying sandwiches.

In a rocking chair on the front veranda, you can calmly reflect on the rich history of this enthralling place where troops were trained on the grounds right out front in 1862. You can imagine Ned Beatty and Patricia Neal rehearsing their lines before walking across the street for a Barter performance. Then you can talk Pete Sheffey into showing you the 200-year-old rosewood bed in the Napoleon Room upstairs or the 1858 Victorian bed given to the inn by silent film star Gloria Swanson. And if you listen intently, after the kitchen closes, you might hear Captain Stover searching for a leftover piece of walnut Italian cream cake in the refrigerator.

The Martha Washington Inn
150 West Main Street
Abingdon, Virginia
(276) 628-9151

Caught Swimming Before Dinner

The Troutdale, Bristol, Tennessee

Every Wednesday a truck full of live trout rolls down Interstate 81 from Flamingo Springs Trout Ponds in Seven Mile Ford, Virginia, on its way to Bristol, Tennessee. The destination is a nineteenth-century spring house on Sixth Street, where a 600-gallon rectangular tank made of concrete teems with Rainbows and Goldens.

Within minutes these mountain trout go from chilly water to hot sauté pan at the Troutdale, voted the Tri-Cities' "most romantic restaurant" by readers of the *Bristol Herald Courier*.

In one eighteen-month period, twenty-four couples became engaged in the candlelit glow of the Troutdale. They often request the same table to celebrate their wedding anniversaries. Surrounded by the deep burgundy walls of the Queen's Room or in the plum-painted Grand Ballroom, with fireplaces flaming throughout this three-story Victorian house, diners mark special events in their lives—new jobs, birthdays, anniversaries.

Romance is the reason Ben Zandi took over the business in September of 2001. A twelve-year Marriott veteran and former vice president for a New England chain of restaurants, Ben met Debra Nickels of Gate City, Virginia, on a cruise in Mexico. Two weeks later they were engaged. Through their Scott County connection Ben and Debra heard about the availability of the Troutdale and purchased the business, fulfilling their dream to escape the corporate world and open a five-star restaurant.

According to the *2003 Guide to Distinguished Restaurants of North America*, "Twenty-seven years of southern fusion cooking have earned this little treasure recognition from leading publications. Trout, kept alive, headline a melting pot menu of European, Asian, and Latin flavors, featuring organic chicken, lamb, duck, veal, beef, game, and seafood" (p. 387).

A simple filet of trout is lightly coated in Parmesan breadcrumbs and sautéed in a butter sauce with capers. Trout Almondine is browned and smothered with butter-toasted almonds and the filets are layered with juli-

Photo courtesy Ben Zandi, The Troutdale.

enned squash, all sitting atop dried-fruit wild rice. For two of the Asian-style trout dishes the fish is served whole. One is breaded and fried in a wok with a sweet chili garlic sauce, while the other is covered with slivered ginger and scallions, poached, sizzled with peanut oil, and drizzled with sesame oil. A third style of trout is rolled. Seasonal trout roulade appears on the menu every evening, including one curled around a stuffing of bacon, mushrooms, and smoked Gouda cheese.

The Troutdale ovens are fragrant with five different breads every day: a Jewish rye loaf, French baguettes, cheese and herb bread, and a cantaloupe-colored sun-dried tomato loaf. All are served with a plate of herbed and spiced extra-virgin olive oil.

Among the dozen appetizers is a baked oyster of the day. The Dynamite Oyster is baked in a garlic-laced, sesame-sprinkled aioli sauce. The Crispy Hoisin-Glazed Shrimp is coated in coarse breadcrumbs and served on a stick with gingered spinach and carrot strings. The shrimp glows with a coating of hoisin sauce, commonly known as Chinese barbecue sauce, its flavor salty from soybeans and sweet from molasses.

The Troutdale employs its own pastry chef, whose creations are as artful as the restaurant's wall paintings rendered by the owner's father. The peanut butter pie was recognized in October 2002 by *Restaurant Hospitality* magazine, but the real luminary of the dessert lineup is the Chocolate Eruption. This masterpiece must be ordered ahead since it involves a twenty-minute baking time. A sweet soufflé, dark in color but light in taste, it is filled with molten chocolate.

The Troutdale serves no frozen products. An organic garden supplies the kitchen in summer, and everything on the menu is homemade. The international wine list is easy to negotiate, categorized according to dryness, lightness, fruitiness, and amount of tannin.

One of the most telling indicators of quality is the presence of the owner. Call for reservations and Ben Zandi is likely to answer the phone. E-mail and he responds personally. During meals he covers every inch of the house, making sure diners are attended to with proper care. One night we even watched him assist a beleaguered parent with a little babysitting.

The Troutdale
412 6th Street
Bristol, Tennessee
(423) 968-9099

Walls of Raisin Torte

The Town House Grill, Chilhowie, Virginia

Tom Bishop knows building. His wife Kyra knows numbers. And Marcus Blackstone knows food. Their combined talents have created a European-style restaurant on otherwise quiet Main Street in the Southwest Virginia town of Chilhowie, population perhaps 2,000.

The Town House is a restaurant that wouldn't be out of place transplanted to a chic street in New York City's SoHo district. Tom and Kyra knew opening such a place in Chilhowie would be a risk, but they considered the proximity to Interstate 81, less than two minutes away, and the short time it takes to drive from cities like Abingdon and Bristol. In 2002 they took their first reservation at the Town House Grill.

Tom, who has worked in building supply sales for over thirty years, designed the copper-bordered birchwood tables. Phyllis Jackson from Blountville, Tennessee, chose "raisin torte" as the paint color for the walls. Kyra, a CPA, set up the books.

After a job in an Atlanta restaurant that required him to cook routinely, Marcus Blackstone excitedly returned to his native Southwest Virginia, cooked a six-course meal for his job interview, and was hired as the first and only chef at the Town House.

Now he has complete freedom in the kitchen. He reduces his barbecue and teriyaki sauces for an Asian glaze to flavor his doorknob-sized, pan-seared sea scallops. He's fashioned a crab cake that holds together with no breading, just egg and garlicky aioli. He's worked up a remoulade sauce worthy of a New Orleans bistro, cooks it into jumbo tiger shrimp, and serves another shot alongside the appetizer in a lemon half.

Filet mignon with sauce espagnole, sashimi-grade Ahi tuna seared with black sesame seeds, grilled lamb chops, chicken marsala, and a 12-ounce Black Angus ribeye are always on the dinner menu. They're supplemented with specials such as sea bass or Tom's favorite, the veal chop, which he

Sesame-seared Ahi tuna. *Photo by Kevin Plowman.*

describes to diners while removing completely cleaned plates from an adjoining table.

Kyra not only takes reservations for the next evening, she also refills water glasses. These aren't absentee owners. They're on the premises all the time, and their watchful but unobtrusive presence accounts for much of the success the Town House has enjoyed.

Their cheery, caring personalities keep employees around. Since the first day Marcus has worked in the kitchen alongside pastry chef Jane Smith, a native of Liverpool, England.

"We've had sticky toffee pudding in Chicago," says Kyra, "but it couldn't touch Jane's." Jane has also brought across the Atlantic an old family recipe for bread-and-butter pudding with homemade cinnamon bread and raisins, cooked in a custard cup with homemade caramel sauce and whipped cream.

Smyth County has long been an apple-growing region, so Kyra says apple pie was a must on the dessert menu. Jane adds a layer of sour cream to the Granny Smith apples—an influence of the Dutch, she says.

There's always a fascinating selection of homemade ice creams, from bergamot-scented scoops made with English Earl Grey tea to ice creams smacking of red velvet cheesecake or mint-chocolate brownies.

The Town House has built one of the most extensive wine lists between Knoxville and Roanoke. In 2004 the restaurant received the *Wine Spectator* Award of Excellence "for having one of the most outstanding restaurant wine lists in the world."

The Town House takes its name from the early designation of the community before the coming of the railroad in 1856, when it was changed to Greever's Switch. That name survives as the title of the filet mignon and lobster tail combination.

A fire wiped out most of the businesses on Main Street in the early 1900s. Before that time the buildings had faced the railroad and the Middle Fork of the Holston River. They were rebuilt and reoriented toward the street with the advent of the automobile.

Small touches come together to create memorable meals at the Town House—a shaving of Peccorino-Romano cheese on roasted potatoes, flecks of tarragon on julienned vegetables, perfectly spaced squirts of bourbon mustard cream topping crab cakes.

"The restaurant business is fun because it's people-oriented, and it gives you instant gratification," says Kyra. "People thank us all the time just for being here."

The Town House Grill
132 East Main Street
Chilhowie, Virginia
(276) 646-8787

Shed the Jacket
and Light the Palm Trees

Café Bonterra, Wise, Virginia

At first there were some who drove past Bonterra in Wise, Virginia, saw the morphed post office, and kept on going for lack of a dinner jacket. Then owner Hugh Belcher, with an intriguing last name for a restaurateur, added breaded mushrooms to the menu, planted three rope-lit plastic palm trees in the front courtyard, and lettered "Café" on the sign. Diners immediately understood. No jacket required.

Café Bonterra is elegance without pretense, sophistication without stiffness. Those fried mushrooms are delivered to the table on Syracuse bone china.

It's a place where children like Jazmin Sturgill forgo French fries for lobster bisque. Jazmin's father, owner of the Lebo Coal Company, says, "It's the best meal I've ever eaten."

"We're close enough friends that he'd sure tell me if it wasn't," retorts Hugh Belcher.

"The people of Wise are ready to name Hugh 'Citizen of the Year' for transforming this place," says Gigi Pippin, president of the local garden club, who as a child had taken piano lessons next door. "This was the ugliest federal government building, and it's so remarkable now. When Hugh started, some of these places on Main Street hadn't been painted in twenty years. Now they've started painting and fixing up, and nobody asked anybody to do it."

With the help of local architect Bill Thompson, iron worker Dean Curfman from Morganton, North Carolina, and artist Sabrina Adams from Wise, the once boxy building became a sage-colored, stuccoed showplace.

The wormy chestnut window casings and the door to the private dining room were constructed using wood salvaged from a Cleveland, Virginia, barn that was about to be burned. The brass-framed marquee inside the front door, which contains a photograph of the original post office building,

Bonterra, Wise, Virginia. *Photo by Fred Sauceman.*

once advertised showings of *Gone with the Wind* at the Fox Theatre in Atlanta, Georgia.

With a putty knife and joint compound Sabrina Adams created a garden of four seasons, painted in a cranberry shade, that completely covers two walls.

"I wanted to create an urban, hip place that offers casual American cuisine," says Hugh, who grew up in Haysi, Virginia.

Diners can adjust their own lighting by raising and lowering maize-shaded lamps centered over each table. Once a week the glass tabletops come off, the television is turned on, and the hot wings are tossed into baskets for college night.

With the closing of Skoby's in Kingsport, Tennessee, chef Bryon Simora, a graduate of the Culinary Institute of America, headed north to Wise and took his place behind Belcher's Vulcan burners.

There he boils down lobster carcasses for his reddish brown bisque, pan-sears yellowfin tuna, and, using the best beef available, builds his Filet Rochelle chock full of lump crabmeat and asparagus and sauces it with Bearnaise.

The old Italian classic *puttanesca*, or "hooker's pasta," studded with whole, briny kalamata olives and sauced tartly with tomatoes, illustrates both the playful attitude of the staff at Bonterra and their respect for the international kitchen.

Hugh Belcher has also taken his turn as experimental bartender, coming up with the Bonterra martini, a citrusy blend of Grand Marnier, Cointreau, vodka, orange juice, and lime.

Diners who crave the corn pudding once offered at the now-closed Skoby's can take comfort in the fact that Chef Bryon has wisely preserved the recipe at Café Bonterra.

Café Bonterra
225 East Main Street
Wise, Virginia
(276) 328-9355

High-Dollar Hash

The Gamekeeper, Boone, North Carolina

Perched on the side of a hill on curvy Shull's Mill Road, a few miles off the picturesque Blue Ridge Parkway in Western North Carolina, The Gamekeeper takes diners back to the aura of a 1940s hunting lodge. It's an era the young owners Wendy and Ken Gordon have only read about.

They spend most of their evenings elbow to elbow inhaling the fragrance of a hickory fire back in the kitchen, where they plate up chutney-coated, sweet-brined boar, fanned filets of ostrich, and bison ribeyes. Elk and pheasant are "specials board" surprises.

All the game is humanely farm-raised, much of it from Colorado. Wendy and Ken are on the "first call" list of fishermen on the coast at Cape Hatteras and Wilmington. These fishermen spear grouper, amberjack, mahi, and triggerfish and ship them to the highlands.

"Speared fish haven't put up a fight, so there's no toughness to the meat," says Ken. He's come a long way from his first restaurant job pushing fast food out the window at a Hardee's, where he once mistook hash browns for filet of fish before another employee set him straight.

Now he's moved from fast-food fries to twice-baked potatoes stuffed with Stilton and goat cheeses. He used a bottle of A.1. as the starting point for his own sun-dried tomato barbecue sauce. Wendy has taken a time-tested chow-chow recipe and sparked it with a liberal sprinkling of cumin and other Indian spices.

"She's always slipping in Asian things," Ken interjects.

"We have a good time. We're not real serious," Wendy adds.

For a special Halloween dinner Ken and Wendy crafted eyeballs out of radishes and stuffed them with olives. They formed mashed-potato ghosts with black-bean eyes and sun-dried tomato devil horns.

A stuffed pheasant peers over the stone fireplace in this 1920s residence and former girls' camp turned restaurant in the mid-1980s, but the game theme is only one part of the restaurant's offerings.

Wendy Gordon in the Gamekeeper kitchen. *Photo by Fred Sauceman.*

Ken and Wendy grill as many vegetables over that hickory fire as they do meat, and they use as much locally grown, organic produce as possible. Organic greens form the bed for a scallop-and-lump-crabmeat croquette topped with Wendy's chow-chow. A grower in Lenoir sells them oyster, chanterelle, and Hen of the Woods mushrooms, and it's not unusual for locals to come in with baskets they've foraged on the mountainsides.

Wendy and Ken jokingly call their fare "high-dollar hash," but they are to be toasted for their reliance on Southern tradition and regional products, comprising what they call "modern mountain cuisine."

"Our first season, we got ramps from Chicago," recalls Wendy. "Now, come June, we use them in everything, and they're all picked right around here."

Cornmeal-coated North Carolina trout is served over collard greens seasoned with strips of Watauga County country ham, alongside a big spoonful of black-eyed peas.

The regional theme carries over to the dessert menu as well. Pear-apple compote and a scoop of homemade butter-pecan ice cream surround a spicy slice of Frangelico-flavored pound cake. Orange-scented homemade doughnuts are served with a cup of hot chocolate for dunking.

Wendy says the busiest month is October, when the "leaf lookers" arrive, but reservations are recommended no matter when you visit. We were there on a bitterly cold January night and the place was completely booked.

After a bowl of prickly pear sorbet in addition to the doughnuts and pound cake, we called a halt to the sweets, but Wendy recommends an evening-ending chocolate martini and a homemade truffle.

The Gamekeeper
3005 Shull's Mill Road
Boone, North Carolina
(828) 963-7400

Samosas and Schnitzel

The Flying Frog Café, Asheville, North Carolina

"Eclectic" is too weak and overused a word to describe a restaurant in Asheville, North Carolina, that can pull off a combination of urban Indian and German cuisines. I'd always wondered how that anomalous match came to be, ever since, back in 1990 at the old Windmill inside the Innsbruck Mall, I changed my order at the last minute from *Wienerschnitzel* to curried mussels.

The Windmill underwent several transformations, the Caribbean-style Latin Quarter among them, and moved to downtown Asheville. In October of 2002 owner Jay Shastri hopped over to the former location of 23 Page, beneath the Haywood Park Hotel, and unveiled the Flying Frog Café.

As it turns out, it was marriage that merged Indian and German on the menu. Jay's first wife Cathie was a German chef, and he's a research chemist from Bombay.

Their son Vijay is executive chef at the Flying Frog and his sister Kirti is director of operations. They have an Italian godmother, who inspired Vijay to make frittatas by age five.

"One morning when Vijay was a little boy, I smelled something sweet, like saffron and cardamom, coming from the kitchen," Jay remembers. "There he was, standing on a chair, making *sheera*, an Indian porridge. I was completely stunned. He said he wanted to surprise me, and a housewife couldn't have made it any better."

Raised on international food, Vijay parlayed his kitchen-sink training into his life's work as a chef. He's had no formal culinary instruction, yet he's learned enough on his own to offer comprehensive wine seminars in the city.

He blends his own curry base, makes his own stocks and chutneys, and boils down the intensely flavored demiglace he uses as a basis for the sauce that covers his *Jägerschnitzel,* a fork-tender German "hunter's cutlet" made of veal and topped with mushrooms.

"We don't hold back on the seasoning and spicing," says Vijay. His *Rotkohl*, German red cabbage, is the sharpest I've encountered, and it's topped with sour cream for added acidity and color contrast.

The Indian appetizer Samosa Tikki mixes potatoes, green peas, raisins, onions, ginger, and spices. It's then dipped in an egg wash, rolled in breadcrumbs, and fried. Homemade date-tamarind chutney and cilantro-ginger chutney accompany the dish.

For the appetizer Tandoori Chicken Tikka, chicken breast meat is marinated in spiced yogurt and grilled, then served with saffron-scented yogurt for dipping.

In a year's time Flying Frog chefs go through about 8 pounds of saffron, a staggering amount considering that it's the world's most expensive spice. Described by Pat Willard as "the world's most seductive spice," saffron is the dried stigmas of the autumn-flowering purple crocus, gathered by hand from the fields of Iran, Greece, Italy, southern France, and Spain.

"Saffron is evocative enough to elicit the most sensuous descriptions," says the dust jacket of Willard's book *Secrets of Saffron.* "Over thousands of years, it has perfumed the halls of Crete's palaces, made Cleopatra more alluring, and driven crusaders and German peasants to their deaths. While many once foreign spices like cinnamon, mace, and ginger no longer spur adventurers to the ends of the earth, saffron remains tantalizingly exotic."

It takes around 210,000 stigmas from 70,000 crocus flowers to yield 1 pound of saffron threads. Spanish saffron scents and seasons the Flying Frog's exceptional Lamb Korma Zaffrani, a creamy, tomato-rich curry with braised lamb shanks. It's one of two Indian lamb dishes that are always on the menu—the other being a vinegary, hot Vindaloo.

The menu doesn't stop at Indian and German. There's an Italian-inspired Lamb Osso Buco, Japanese Kobe beef, a Southern crab cake with Louisiana French remoulade sauce, and pan-seared North Carolina mountain trout. Roast duckling is served with a brandied blackberry-port wine sauce, and sourwood honey from Yancey County is used as a glaze for grilled pork tenderloin. Sushi-grade tuna is dusted with mortar-ground sesame seeds and black peppercorns.

The menu is devoid of frog legs, and there's no cultural significance to the airborne amphibian theme other than the fact that, as Jay says, "Frogs are international; frogs are everywhere." The name was the result of a spontaneous doodling session.

The Flying Frog and the Frog Bar and Deli upstairs mix all manner of funky drinks—the Flirtini with raspberry vodka, the Dirty Cajun with pepper vodka and olive juice, the Gingertini blending vanilla vodka and fresh ginger syrup, and a mimosa made from the juice of the lychee fruit. Kirti says the martinis made with lychee juice have a "rosy nose."

"Asheville is going to be an international destination," predicts Jay. "I've been saying that since the 1980s. Many people didn't believe me, but many people also told me I couldn't make it running a restaurant that served Indian and German food, either."

Jay says the new owner of the Haywood Park plans to convert it into an art-deco boutique hotel. "This is the perfect corner for us," Jay adds, as the glass candleholder at our table spontaneously cracks into two pieces from the heat. "In India, when the glass breaks, that's a good sign."

The Flying Frog Café
1 Battery Park
Asheville, North Carolina
(828) 254-9411

Kingsport's Quiche Queens
Two Sisters Tea Room and Gifts, Kingsport, Tennessee

Norma Bevins has poured her personality into the tea room business. For thirty-five years she was steeped in secretarial work at Holston Defense in Kingsport, Tennessee. Now she's sweetened up a 1935 house in the city's Colonial Heights neighborhood, turning it into the Two Sisters Tea Room and Gifts.

An interior decorator asked Norma where she'd learned to fix up a house like that, with lavender and purple walls in one room and a border of teacup-covered wallpaper in another. Norma stirred the visitor up a bit by admitting she'd had no training—just as she'd never run a restaurant before bravely taking over the tea room in 2002.

She's even charmed the Presbyterians across the street into a shared parking lot agreement.

From Cracker Barrel gift shops to antique emporiums, Norma searches out additions for the walls and tables, touches like the porcelain napkin rings resembling small teapots. She and Carolyn McNutt, her friend of forty years, greet guests from behind an antique round-dial Zenith radio converted into a hostess station.

Despite tea room frills and dainty décor, there's solid sustenance here. Norma's quiche selections are fortified with goodly portions of sour cream, mayonnaise, and half and half. There's a chicken-pecan; a traditional, oniony Lorraine; and a hearty broccoli-bacon.

The Two Sisters clientele is largely female, but Norma knew more business from the male gender was brewing recently when five men from Eastman Chemical Company walked in clamoring for quiche.

A mainstay on the menu is almond chicken casserole, served hot. The moderately thick tomato and dill soup is adapted from a tea room in Mississippi.

Norma Bevins and Carolyn McNutt. *Photo by Fred Sauceman.*

Muffins are usually commonplace on tea room menus, but instead Two Sisters offers a square of Scottish shortbread sprinkled with powdered sugar, saved by some customers for dessert.

Norma borrowed the idea for her signature dessert, Heavenly Delight, from a restaurant in Charleston, South Carolina. She's improved upon it by making her own waffle cone, stuffing it inside a glass bowl, and then, in free-form fashion, filling it with ice cream, caramel, seasonal fruits, and chocolate, raspberry, and pineapple syrups, all smothered in whipped cream.

Coca-Colas are brought to the table in bottles, with a glass of ice.

"I'm still amazed that people pay to eat my food," says Norma. In her former life she spent her days fielding phone calls, filing documents, arranging meetings, and circulating memoranda, the kind of detailed work that prepared her well for her second career as a self-taught tea room proprietor.

Two Sisters Tea Room and Gifts
216 Colonial Heights Road
Kingsport, Tennessee
(423) 239-5657

5

From the Sugar Sack

We bead up the Adirondack,
crack horehound, approach divinity,
and forgo fallout.

The "House Wine of the South"

Ice Tea at High Summer

Like the splash of cannonball dives in neighborhood swimming pools, the ring of metal bats in raucous sandlot softball games, and the creaking of rockers on aging wooden porches, ice tea means summer in the South.

Tall glasses of the deep-amber liquid, accented and flavored with lemon and mint and sweetened with white sugar, accompany checkered-cloth picnics on roadside tables, sit alongside plates of smoky pork barbecue in cinder block restaurants, and slowly sweat on the wide arms of Adirondack chairs during late afternoon breaks from the garden.

One evening during pre-Dog Days, I heard Fred Thompson on National Public Radio's "All Things Considered" describe the ideal way to prepare the perfect pitcher of Southern sweet tea. This Fred Thompson is not our Tennessee politician-turned-actor, who probably also makes a noble tea in addition to replicating his mother's coconut cream pie and coconut cake.

The Fred Thompson who was conversing with NPR's Susan Stamberg that evening is a food writer, and he has compiled entire books on lemonade, ice tea, and crabs. His words "baking soda" caught my attention and I fished pen and paper out of the glove compartment. In my own shorthand I took down every detail of his method and later bought the book, *Iced Tea*, at a local Kroger.

"It's high summer; it's time to think beyond the woes of this world, the Middle East, the bumpy market, and get to the really important stuff, the perfect glass of iced tea," said Stamberg as she introduced the radio segment, with Thompson on the phone from Myrtle Beach, South Carolina.

Thompson's way of making the "house wine of the South" goes like this. Put six regular-size tea bags in a heat-proof container—I have a gray pottery bowl with a handle on it, made by my aunt, and I dedicate it to this one operation only. Sprinkle over the tea bags a good pinch of baking soda, which Thompson says will smooth out the tannin in the tea and eliminate

Ice tea at high summer. Photo by Larry Smith.

the bitterness. Pour two cups of boiling water over the tea bags, cover the container, and steep for fifteen minutes. Remove the tea bags from the liquid but do not squeeze them. Pour the concentrate into a heat-proof pitcher along with anywhere from a cup to 1 1/2 cups of sugar, stir, and add 6 cups of cold water. Stir well and let cool to room temperature. Do not refrigerate until the tea is completely cool or it will become cloudy. To serve, I squeeze a chunk of lemon over the ice in a glass, drop in the lemon, pour in the tea, add a sprig of fresh mint, and inhale. All told it's about a twenty-minute process, quicker than a trip to the store for a canned or plastic-bottled substitute.

This has become our "house tea," endorsed by my mother, who describes it as exactly the color of my grandmother's. One can aspire to many things in life, but I can think of few better and more fulfilling achievements than to make tea like your grandmother's.

Speaking of tea, is it "iced tea," or "ice tea"? Thompson says it depends on where you were raised. Growing up in North Carolina, he never added the "d." It's a cosmopolitan affectation but one that has become so universally accepted that he was forced to insert the "d" into the title of his ninety-six-page book. John Shelton Reed and Dale Volberg Reed, in their book *1001 Things Everyone Should Know About the South*, leave off the "d."

Some theorize that Southerners' love of sweet tea had its origins in barbecue houses and fish camps at a time when sugar was cheaper to buy than tea. Excessive amounts of sugar were added to "stretch" the beverage, so the story goes. Alabama writer Rick Bragg likens unsweetened tea to "a glass of brown water."

Thompson's brand of choice is Luzianne, and he stashes several boxes into his suitcase before spending part of each year in Manhattan "to ensure that I have quality tea."

In her non-fiction work *Consuming Passions: A Food-Obsessed Life*, novelist Michael Lee West writes of ice tea, "It's the backbone of summer, especially when served with pecan chicken salad and garden tomatoes."

An End-of-Summer
Salutation to Lemonade

Lemonade is one of summer's most memorable and enduring symbols, and food writer Fred Thompson has not only swilled it, he's studied it.

Growing up in North Carolina, Thompson counted the days until the third Sunday in September. He'd look forward to the annual family reunion all year. He reveled in fried chicken and cornbread, but it was the lemonade that left the most lasting impression and led him to write an entire book on the subject.

"My grandmother, my dad's mother, her side of the family, they were Daughtreys, and they got together in an old community building. A group of men took an old wooden washtub, and then it became a galvanized washtub, and made lemonade from scratch. They would start about six o'clock in the morning and hand-squeeze every lemon, and they always threw the lemon rinds in, to get more of those essential oils out. That was the best lemonade I ever had, and still probably, in my food memory, the best lemonade there ever will be."

In America, lemonade has come to be identified both with leisure and ambition. Thompson says his favorite place to down a glass is on the boardwalk of a Southern beach at sunset. And, for many fellow baby boomers, a lemonade stand was their first brush with entrepreneurship, their first lesson in counting change, a step toward independence, even though mothers and fathers monitored transactions out kitchen windows. Lemonade stands taught lessons in handling disappointment when pedestrians and passing cars offered no more than a wave of the hand and most of the product was carted back home for parents to buy.

Thompson notes a Mason-Dixon Line difference in preferences for sweet-sour balance in a glass of lemonade.

"I was born and raised in the South, and my judgment of lemonade is probably a little different from someone who was born in Manhattan, for instance. And having had a lot of lemonade in Manhattan, there is a huge difference. They like it much tarter than I do. I want a sweet start, with a tart kick at the end. It's personal taste. Freshness is the one thing that makes a great glass of lemonade. Freshly squeezed juice."

I asked Thompson to take us through the produce section of the grocery store and tell us what to look for in buying lemons.

"Look for ugly lemons. I'm a food stylist so part of my job is putting beautiful looking produce in front of a camera for photographs, but, typically, beautiful things don't taste very good. Look for small lemons. They tend to have more juice. The larger lemons are all for show."

He points out that lemons are always cheaper in January and February when we don't really think about drinking lemonade.

"In July, they're kind of expensive—two for a dollar—and so what I'll do a lot of times is buy lemons in January and juice them. I want to get about two cups of lemon juice, four cups of water, and two cups of sugar, and mix all that together. You really wind up with a kind of slurry because with that much sugar, it won't ever totally freeze hard. Put it in a container, stick it in the freezer, and wait for that first 85-degree day in June. Pull it out, and then use half concentrate to half water."

Except for maybe chocolate cake, Thompson says he can't think of many foods that don't go well with lemonade.

"I think lemonade works well with all the different types of Southern barbecue, from Texas to North Carolina to Memphis to the panhandle of Florida. It works really well with fried chicken, because the acidity helps cut any greasiness that's in there. It's the perfect thing for a lot of what we consider basic Southern foods."

Thompson is just as knowledgeable about the history of lemons.

"The lemon was a by-product of the Crusades," he tells me. "The Crusaders brought it back from the Middle East. It turned out that the juice was pretty good for preventing scurvy, so it quickly became an essential thing on most sailing vessels. According to one tale, Columbus was served lemonade when he visited Queen Isabella to get his finances together for his trip to the New World. Some people think France started drinking lemonade in the 1600s. Here in the United States, it was probably a French pharmacist in the 1830s who actually developed a drink we now call lemonade."

Thompson estimates he juiced around 3,400 lemons experimenting with the 50 recipes that eventually made it into his book, *Lemonade*.

He says lemonade's a beverage that has become the victim of our ever-quickening pace, with powdered belly wash, reconstituted lemon juice, and canned versions dominating the market.

But Thompson believes making fresh lemonade is therapeutic, from the hand exercise you get if you use a non-mechanical, non-electric squeezer, to the relaxing wait for the sugar syrup to cool.

Fred Thompson is also the author of *Iced Tea*, and lest you think he's only a hot weather beverage scholar, he's now finishing up a book about hot chocolate.

A Solution for Runny Honey

Knoxville's Honeyberry Farm

"What you see here is a circle that's all first cousins and aunts and uncles. It's 30 acres in the midst of suburban West Knoxville, the remnants of my grandfather's farm. His grandfather's grandfather purchased it in 1806, and we've been on this land ever since."

In the midst of summer, Brenda Hubbell's home place, Honeyberry Farm, is a "bee-loud glade," to quote the Irish poet William Butler Yeats, even though it's a short shot off noisy Northshore Drive.

A food technologist, Brenda put in her time with Stouffer's Frozen Foods, Tastykake in Philadelphia, with frozen food magnate Banquet, and as a lobbyist for the Frozen Food Association.

Then she came back home to East Tennessee and followed a dream. Not a dream of the youthful, innocent, starry-eyed variety. A real, REM-stage, fast asleep, head on the pillow dream.

Her uncle was a beekeeper, and one night, she dreamed she put his bees in a field of clove basil and got clove-flavored honey. He explained to her how you can't make bees do anything against their will.

Yet she was determined to tweak Mother Nature and outdo the Smucker's corporation at the same time. Like a lot of breakfast-time honey-eaters, she wished for a way to make the product less runny. A salesman had taken her to lunch to give her a sales pitch for a new kind of gum, stronger than the jelling agent pectin and capable of holding more sugar in its molecular matrix.

"Gellan gum, the agent I use, is made from the cell wall of a bacterium," says Brenda. "It's pasteurized and harvested, and it acts exactly like pectin does, which is what's in Sure-Jell, but it's stronger, allowing me to make my jellies anywhere from 70 to 90 percent honey."

Brenda discovered Smucker's owned the patent on honey jelled with pectin, but it ended at a lower sugar content than she was producing with the new gum. She applied for and was granted a patent that upped the sugar percentage in the jelly.

Photo by Larry Smith.

Brenda, her father, A. C. Camp, and her sister, Connie Ford, built a jelly kitchen between their houses, and they've been turning out honey jelly, sometimes as many as 500 jars a day, for a decade. Brenda uses commercial honey, clover from around the country and orange blossom from Florida. The honey's pasteurized before she gets it, and to make the jelly, she heats it to 150 degrees, so there's a double shot of protection against bacteria and mold. The label advises refrigeration after the product is opened, but Brenda says it does just fine at room temperature.

The operation's rural location is advantageous. Brenda discovered that the honey won't jell with city water.

"And not all honey will jell," she adds. "The jelling agent is mineral sensitive, and each lot of honey differs."

With its smooth texture, customers often prefer honey jelly spooned right out of the jar, but Brenda and her family have devised a number of serving options. They say the peach and pear flavors are best on hot biscuits.

"My grandmother insisted on Georgia Belle peaches for her peach preserves, and I would sit beside her eating the ripe skin peelings that she was preparing," Brenda recalls. "I chose this peach flavor from my memory, added a little cinnamon and amaretto, and made the jelly for a hot, buttered biscuit."

For bagels and cream cheese, the best match is raspberry, Brenda's favorite because of the balance between honey and berry flavor. Orange blossom and cinnamon go well atop toasted English muffins. Rosemary balsamic, made with rosemary harvested out of Brenda's garden, is good over lamb chops and pork tenderloin or poured into a baked sweet potato. Some customers glaze chicken with it.

And then there's pecan. It's Honeyberry Farm's best seller, combining clover honey, Georgia pecans, and brown sugar. It can turn a piece of plain toast into a sticky bun.

Brenda's sister Connie bakes a chocolate sheet cake, and while it's cooling, she brings to a boil half a jar of pecan honey jelly and a quarter jar of water. She breaks the cake into pieces, pours the heated jelly over them, and sprinkles in some pecans.

"And everybody always has some vanilla ice cream at home," says Connie. "When company comes, take a little bit of the jelly, stir it up, pour it over the ice cream, and you've got the best ice cream sundae you've ever eaten. Maybe with a little whipped cream."

Once too shy to greet visitors at wholesale booths, Brenda now parades around in a queen bee outfit at festivals and fairs, handing out white plastic spoons and plugging a new approach to one of the world's oldest and most nutritious foods, now a little less drippy.

Honeyberry Farms
Knoxville, Tennessee
(865) 539-2512

A Fried-Pie Fiefdom

Seaver's Bakery, Johnson City, Tennessee

Fried pies, in rows of eight on a conveyor belt, weave an hour-long, serpentine trek around the second floor of Seaver's Bakery in Johnson City, Tennessee. By the time they crawl up to the third story, the crimped, half-moon confections are cool and ready to be slipped into glassine packages.

The family recipe and the fillings haven't changed since O. R. Seaver opened the bakery in 1949. Richard McKinney was hired as a route salesman seven years later, and he's still there today, as plant manager.

"The majority of fried pies have a sugar glaze on them," he tells me in response to my question about the qualities that make a good Tennessee fried pie. "Once that glazed sugar goes on, which we do not put on our pies, it takes away the taste of the pie and you taste more sugar than you do fruit. That's the reason consumers like our pies, because they're not sugar-coated."

Richard says old-timers like him are partial to raisin fried pies, but the number-one selling Seaver's pie, two to one, is apple, made from dried, steam-cooked Granny Smiths.

Along with seven other flavors, they're dumped into a trough of 380-degree vegetable oil, 16 inches deep, where they bob for three and a half minutes before popping onto the belt on the other side, completely dry.

The bakery turns out pies under a Seaver's label and a Kern's label. The products are identical, but Richard says some customers insist there's a difference.

The days of route sales are gone. Pies are now sold at convenience markets, a few thrift stores, and newsstands. Though the office manager's eighty-seven years old, the packer's seventy-six, and the plant manager's seventy, Seaver's Bakery is more than a relic from the days when the word "fried" got no frowns. Lucrative deals are in process with grocery store and discount chains, ready for a fried pie revival.

Seaver's Bakery
3300 Mayfield Drive
Johnson City, Tennessee
(423) 928-8131

Doughnut Devotion

Krispy Kreme in Dutch

"Do you think they'll let us on the plane with these?" The two ladies in front of me at the Krispy Kreme Doughnut store in Kingsport, Tennessee, debated the idea briefly and decided to take their chances with 3 dozen, mostly the original glazed variety, plus a few topped with red, white, and blue sprinkles.

These two enthusiastic customers, one American and one Dutch, trace their ties back to a World War II-era romance. Helena Schelberg met John Wallace, Sr., as his outfit was clearing the streets of Nazis in Sittard, located in The Netherlands. Family reunions in West Virginia and doughnut devotion have kept their descendants close ever since.

When Dorothy Buscher, an elementary school teacher in Sittard, and her family spent three weeks visiting Delores Wallace and her family in Kingsport, they made five trips to Krispy Kreme for 2 dozen doughnuts at a time and once for 3 dozen.

Dorothy came to America with a goal of visiting a Krispy Kreme store, since she'd only had the doughnuts off a grocery shelf in West Virginia, says Delores Wallace. "I said I could do better than that. I can show you where they make them, and we stayed in the store about an hour."

They watched as a conveyor belt clearly visible to every customer transported Dorothy's favorite, the original glazed, through the steps from dough to doughnut to counter. They were amazed to learn from supervisor Harry Barrow that the Kingsport store alone produces 4,000 to 5,000 dozen doughnuts every day.

"The plain glazed ones just melt in your mouth," says Dorothy. "They're smooth, unlike Dutch doughnuts."

Although tall and trim, on trip number five to Krispy Kreme Dorothy said she had great concerns about buckling the seatbelt on the plane ride back home.

Krispy Kreme traces its origins back to the midst of the Great Depression. In 1933 Vernon Rudolph bought a doughnut shop in Paducah,

Dorothy Buscher and Delores Wallace stick together through a transatlantic admiration of Krispy Kreme doughnuts. *Photo by Larry Smith.*

Kentucky, from a New Orleans French chef. He and his partner soon moved their operations to Nashville, where the business primarily involved selling doughnuts to local grocery stores. In 1937 Rudolph and two other young men loaded their doughnut-making equipment into their 1936 Pontiac, pooled their $200, and headed east, eventually settling in Winston-Salem, North Carolina, land of tobacco and textiles.

The partners spent their last $25 to rent a building near Salem College, convinced a local grocer to lend them ingredients for their first batch of doughnuts, and removed the back seat of the Pontiac to install a delivery rack. On July 13, 1937, the first Krispy Kreme doughnuts were sold.

The demand for hot doughnuts was so great that Rudolph opened the shop for retail business by cutting a hole in the wall. Thus began the first modern-day window service.

Krispy Kreme has become such a strong force in American culinary culture that in 1997 company artifacts were inducted into the Smithsonian Institution's National Museum of American History.

The company's devotion to education is almost as well known throughout America as its illuminated "Hot Doughnuts Now" signs. The children at River Valley Christian School in Fort Smith, Arkansas, raised over $100,000 for scholarships through Friday doughnut sales.

As a member of Friends of Krispy Kreme, I'm notified monthly about new store openings across the country. Bridgeville, Pennsylvania, population 5,445, now has a Krispy Kreme store, as does Riverhead, New York, population 27,680. My home of Johnson City, Tennessee, with a population of almost 60,000, has a new restaurant named after the Duke of Wellington but no Krispy Kreme store of its own. I'm restricted almost solely to convenience store sales in my pursuit of the chocolate-iced, creme-filled variety—"a yeast-raised doughnut shell," says the corporate description, "hand-filled with rich, smooth white creme and then carefully topped off with a coating of chocolate icing."

It's decadence for under a dollar.

"You Don't Walk in Off the Street and Do This"

Helms Candy Company, Bristol, Virginia

In this time of bulging Christmas lists and marathon shopping binges, when the entire holiday seems like a competition to spend more, wrap more, and get more, it's important to remember that for many children in the Appalachian Mountain region December 25 meant one gift.

Oftentimes, that gift was a box of candy, in a simple, rectangular, stark white box, with a bold red stripe around it, and a window of cellophane across the top. Pure sugar stick candy from the Moretz Candy Company in Bristol, Virginia, brightened many an otherwise bleak Christmas for countless children in the Appalachian Mountains. George and Duke Moretz founded the company in a Bristol, Virginia garage over seventy years ago and sold candy in the coal fields. In 2005, the business was acquired by an even older enterprise, Helms Candy Company, also located in Bristol.

Frank Helms, Sr., founded the company in 1909, and it's still owned and operated by the Helms family. Richard Gibian, Jr., originally from Selma, Alabama, is general manager. His family has been in the candy-making business for 100 years. Richard samples candy all day long but is, as we say in the mountains, thin as a rail, a condition he attributes to "high metabolism."

While many customers buy Red Band Candy for a nostalgic remembrance of Christmases past, its producers have kept up with the modern marketplace. Red Band now sells soft peppermint candy puffs, which can be purchased individually in stores. And a Colorado company is selling the porous Red Band candy sticks as "iced tea sippers." For years, people have used the candy as a straw to extract the juice from oranges and lemons. Another concession to modern-day consumerism: in large letters, on every box, the words "Fat Free."

Some cooks grind up the candy and use it for cake decorations, and you can plop a vanilla-flavored puff into your morning coffee.

Moretz Candy Company, Bristol, Virginia. *Photo by Larry Smith.*

In the wintertime, customers show up on the doorstep of the business in Bristol to buy horehound sticks. They're all natural and flavored with the slightly bitter herb that many claim has medicinal properties. Horehound is an old-time mountain remedy for colds.

The primary product, though, is still the striped, peppermint-flavored, pure sugar stick candy.

The manufacturing facility houses its share of digital thermometers, conveyor belts, and even metal detectors to make sure the final product is free of foreign material, but the making of Red Band candy is still largely done by hand.

Sugar and water are cooked in copper kettles over open fire, and the 300-degree liquid is water-cooled on a steel slab. That 100-pound batch is pulled, which introduces air and turns the product white. Flavoring is added to the white portion, not to the stripes, as some people assume.

Stripes are pieces of candy that don't get pulled, and the color is achieved by mixing in various powders. On the day of our visit, employees were making sassafras sticks, with orange and green striping. After going through a series of rollers, 15-foot ropes of candy emerge.

Wendy Whitaker, a former softball player, slings those ropes down a cornstarch-covered belt, and each one comes to rest at the exact same point. Those 15-foot ropes are then chopped into sticks and boxed. A 12-ounce white-and-red box usually contains about forty-five sticks.

Richard Gibian says you don't walk in off the street and make this kind of candy. It's almost a lost art that requires practice and patience.

There have been refinements along the way and a few new products added to the line, like a key lime-flavored puff in 2005, but the Helms family learned early on how devoted people in Southern Appalachia are to the company's peppermint stick candy and they've never changed the taste.

It's a symbol of Yuletide simplicity worth celebrating all year long.

Helms Candy Company, Inc.
3001 Lee Highway
Bristol, Virginia
(276) 669-2612

A Bachelor Button Bastion

The Peggy Ann Bakery and Deli, Greeneville, Tennessee

First there's a cloud of powdered sugar, then the shattering of puff pastry and a glossy cushion of buttercream. Cream horns from the Peggy Ann Bakery in Greeneville, Tennessee, are a triumvirate of textures.

The Peggy Ann is an independently owned bakery, not a part of a grocery store conglomerate. Even when the business was located in the old Super Dollar, precursor to the regional Food City chain, Peggy and Bill Arrowood made it their own place. They turned out their first cherry-topped sweet rolls at the Snapps Ferry Road store in 1956, and three years later they'd sold enough doughnuts, birthday cakes, and bachelor buttons to buy the business. In those early days Peggy worked without a salary.

Today the bakery is a mother-son operation. Bill died in 1988 and the Arrowoods' son John, who studied bakery science and management at Kansas State University, runs the business with his wife Imogene, who follows in her mother-in-law's footsteps as a master cake decorator.

Peggy iced baseball diamonds on my childhood birthday cakes and sold my mother our daily breakfast bread—"salt-risen," always pronounced with a long "i." My mother could slice that bread so thin you'd swear she'd buttered it on both sides.

"Salt-risen is probably one of the best breads people can eat as far as fat content and sugar content go," says John. "It starts out with a scalded cornmeal base and milk, and you boil it and let it set overnight to make it sour. Then you add another stage to it. It's a three-stage process. You have to let it sour some more. It's like a real old-fashioned sourdough bread, with scalded cornmeal instead of flour. When you're making it, the more it stinks, the better it's going to be. It's a real tight, firm-textured bread."

The Peggy Ann's number-one selling cookie is the bachelor button. John and his staff bake about 200 dozen a week—some colored yellow and black for Chuckey-Doak High School class reunions, some matched with wedding colors, some in baby-shower pink, some lavender for the spring Iris Festival

Imogene, Peggy, and John Arrowood assemble Chocolate Delight. *Photo by Larry Smith.*

or orange for University of Tennessee tailgating. It's a shortbread cookie filled with a disk of colored fondant icing made of egg whites and powdered sugar.

"Some people call them thumb cookies," says John, "but I don't use my thumb. I use my forefinger."

There's hardly a graduation party, bridal shower, or retirement bash in town without at least one item from the Peggy Ann, be it a plate of finger rolls stuffed with chicken salad, a basket of butterflake rolls, or a platter of Danish pastries.

"Greeneville's a very sociable town, a partying town," says John. "They like to celebrate everything here. They spend a lot of money on entertaining where a lot of towns don't. Plants, factories, schools—they like to party down, and that's very unique."

On a "normal" day the Peggy Ann sells 100 dozen doughnuts, beginning around 6 A.M. Some twelve to fifteen varieties are available daily, including custard-filled Boston creams, blueberry cake, strawberry cake, lemon-filled, raspberry-filled, chocolate-covered, and plain glazed. The chocolate-covered, cream-filled doughnut is sliced in half and the cream ladled inside. I went home and weighed one—8 ounces.

Of the ideal doughnut John says, "I want it to firm up good and be soft in the middle, with a tender flake and tender bite. They're all natural rise, no steam, no pressure."

During a typical week the Peggy Ann bakes enough cake to feed 8,000 people. From the Super Dollar days in the 1960s I remember round chocolate cakes 6 inches across. John has taken the basic elements of those cakes and reassembled them into the individually portioned Chocolate Delight, a rectangle of chocolate cake, a cylinder of buttercream icing, and a latticework of quick-hardening chocolate sauce.

Peggy ices up a United States flag for an American Legion sheet cake while Imogene creates a tropical scene on another, parrot and all, using a cocktail napkin as a guide.

From the sugar cookies to the prune cake, everything is baked in the same type of oven the Arrowoods used fifty years ago.

"Bakers are dying out," says John. "It's physical, hot work, with long hours on your feet. If you love slipping off for three-day weekends, this is not the job for you. And holidays are your biggest times.

"Salesmen come through here all the time and tell me there's not a place like this between here and Atlanta."

The Peggy Ann Bakery and Deli
934 Snapps Ferry Road
Greeneville, Tennessee
(423) 639-1924

Cinnamon Rolls off the Interstate

The Wildflour Bakery, Abingdon, Virginia

In 1792 a deed is issued for a parcel of Southwest Virginia property. A little over a hundred years later James David Campbell cuts his own timber from the land and finishes his farmhouse. Skip forward almost exactly a century and the wife of Campbell's great-grandson accomplishes something equally monumental.

Out on the back porch Donna McIntyre turns out the first pan of cinnamon rolls from the new location of the Wildflour Bakery. Donna's family has been known around Abingdon, Virginia, for dough dexterity since 1972, when they opened the popular Bella's Pizza on the historic town's East Main Street.

In the 1970s Donna's sister-in-law's sister Lori Brehm trekked cross-country from Berkeley, California, to offer lessons on croissant dough and puff pastry. Swathed in early-morning baking aromas for years, Donna's husband Tom told her, "If you bake, they'll come."

So in 1997 the McIntyres moved their baking business to the old pine-floored farmhouse, once the site of a noisy sawmill. That croissant dough, buttered, sugared, and spiced, became the basis for the Wildflour's cinnamon rolls, baked and glazed every day. Diners' love of Donna's bearclaws, blueberry muffins, and scones soon prompted them to start asking, "What's for lunch?" Mid-day soup from scratch with bread and butter evolved in 2003 into blackened salmon and shrimp scampi dinners.

About the time that original deed for the Campbell property was issued, White's Mill opened near Abingdon. Much to the delight of Wildflour chef Roger Goodson, today this eighteenth-century business is still grinding grits and supplying his kitchen.

"It's a better, heartier, coarser ground grit than I've found anywhere else in the South," Roger says.

Roger blends smoked Gouda cheese and chopped scallions with these locally produced grits to create his favorite side dish. Although the Wildflour

Donna McIntyre finishes off a sheet of chocolate chip cookies. *Photo by Murray Lee, MurrayLee.com.*

menu does change periodically, smoked-Gouda grits is a permanent dinner accompaniment.

Sides like cheese grits and roasted-garlic sweet potatoes are emblematic of Roger's kitchen philosophy. He's the owner of eleven black-iron skillets and one small microwave, which he uses only for melting butter.

"I want this place to be just like home, with very simple foods, no 3-foot-tall garnishes and shaved fennel," says Roger. "It's so casual here, people will walk right into the kitchen to compliment us after a meal."

Although the Bloody Mary Shrimp sounds like a British schoolyard insult, it's one of Roger's most requested appetizers. He had a pitcher of Bloody Mary on hand one night, mixed a few glugs with some shrimp, and seared them until the tomatoey liquid permeated and coated the shellfish.

Roger, who got his first kitchen job at the Lee Highway Howard Johnson, says he's always been fascinated by food and constantly offered to help his grandparents prepare meals.

Multi-generational influence is evident throughout the Wildflour. Donna McIntyre's great-grandmother Mary Gay lived until Donna was in the sixth grade. She always had a loaf of New York's Lancaster Town Bakery bread, with a nice dark crust, on the table.

"Grandma Gay made two pies for every Sunday dinner," remembers Donna. "And the children asked for a piece of each."

Grandma Gay was known for her fruit pies in a custard base. Undoubtedly she would approve of her great-granddaughter's strawberry tart with its layers of chocolate, cream cheese, and puréed strawberries.

Wildflour Bakery is a muffin's throw off rumbling Interstate 81, but you'd never know it out back around the old smokehouse.

The Wildflour Bakery
Just off Interstate 81, exit 19
Abingdon, Virginia
(276) 676-4221

Sugary Architecture

The National Gingerbread House Competition and Display, Asheville, North Carolina

Christina Banner sees the domes atop St. Basil's Cathedral in Moscow's Red Square and thinks of Hershey's Kisses. London's Big Ben conjures up images of sugar wafers. Mention the North Pole and her attention turns to Rice Krispies Treats.

Christina is architect, interior designer, structural engineer, and construction worker. Her building materials come from the candy counter and the grocery store. Her medium is gingerbread.

In the fall of 2004 she baked, molded, tinted, shaped, and iced her way to the very top of the gingerbread universe, winning the grand prize in the National Gingerbread House Competition sponsored by the Grove Park Inn Resort and Spa in Asheville, North Carolina.

Starting out with a dozen strictly Western North Carolina entries in 1993, the competition has mushroomed to more than 225 from all across the country. Diane Sawyer was the first to use the term "national" to describe the competition on ABC's *Good Morning America,* which has hosted the winners since 1998, their delicate creations carefully hauled by automobile to Manhattan. Any minor damage is repaired at the last minute with squirts of royal icing, a blend of egg whites and powdered sugar.

Royal icing is to the gingerbread house maker as mortar is to the brick mason, with one notable exception. It's edible, as everything else on, inside, or around the gingerbread creations must be.

Gingerbread judges are generally kind souls who get misty and poetic about the warmth of the season and holiday memories—but leave the stick in your lollipop tree or the string inside your rock-candy icicle and it's immediate, unequivocal disqualification from the competition.

"Judging is always tricky, but we're looking for details, animation, and a lot of depth to the houses, so the more you look at them, the more you dis-

Christina Banner's winning gingerbread entry, "Christmas Around the World." *Photo by Fred Sauceman.*

cover," says Aaron Morgan, executive pastry chef at the Grove Park and lead judge.

Christina's winning entry, "Christmas Around the World," was five-sided and built on a swivel, so every panel had to be as detailed as the other.

"Each side represented that country's vision of Christmas," she said. "Inside each window was a dessert that country would serve for Christmas— panettone, a Christmas bread with icing and sprinkles, for Italy, a Yule log for France, Christmas pudding for England, and a braided kolach with a candle on top to represent Russia."

She struggled the hardest to come up with one dessert symbolic of the various cuisines of America, finally settling on a milk-and-cookies reward for Santa Claus.

She manufactured a crown and torch for the Statue of Liberty, engineered a Leaning Tower of Pisa for Italy, sculpted the multicolored onion domes for the Russian cathedral, transformed the crisscross pattern of sugar wafers into the exterior of London's Big Ben, and stayed up far into the night modeling a fragile Parisian Eiffel Tower out of gingerbread.

"I'm really, truly amazed at the workmanship and the creativity and the vast variety of different designs and ideas, from little houses to churches that are opened up so you can see the organ inside to barns to Rock City, to a large teapot, to Diagon Alley from the Harry Potter books," comments Sylvia Holmes, a native of Yorkshire, England, who travels to Asheville yearly from her home outside Charlotte to see the exhibit. "Half of the fun is looking to see what materials have been used, little squares of cereals for roof tiles, pretzels for fencing, in addition to all of the icing and the rich colors."

Brenden Biddix of Leicester, North Carolina, crafted a palm tree out of waffled ice cream cones to shade Santa Claus, who sipped a tropical drink out of a coconut. Entries ran the gamut from Joey Summer's Redneck Christmas, complete with outhouse, rusted-out automobile, and moonshine still, to Trish McCallister's graceful, columned antebellum mansion.

In an offbeat blend of holidays, the roof of one house was decked with pink, purple, and yellow Peeps from the Easter season and on the front wall were marshmallowy Halloween ghosts and black cats.

"We saw some Slim Jims this year, so we've actually got some meat products in the gingerbread, used for pillars on a doghouse," says Chef Morgan, a Johnson and Wales University graduate who runs a pre-competition gingerbread emergency room to repair any sagging shutters or detached doors.

"You have to love to play around and get frustrated," adds Christina. "If you don't love getting frustrated, don't even try it."

A gingerbread competition at the Grove Park was the idea of current president and CEO James Craig Madison, the resort's marketing director in the early 1990s. Until 1984 the Grove Park stayed closed for six months out of the year. The management was seeking out ways to bring in more visitors during the winter months and at the same time the decorations budget for the sprawling inn had dwindled, so Madison devised the gingerbread competition as a cost-free way to make the resort feel more like Christmas.

"It conjures up all those great memories of Christmas past that didn't have anything to do with commercialization or what kind of presents you were going to get," says the resort's public relations manager Phil Werz. "It's all about your imagination and letting it run wild."

One guest remarked, "I'm kicking myself for not bringing my camera."

The National Gingerbread House Display is open seven days a week, twenty-four hours a day, from mid-November through early January.

The Grove Park Inn
Resort and Spa
290 Macon Avenue
Asheville, North Carolina
(800) 438-5800

Time for Ice Cream

The Tic-Toc Ice Cream Parlor, Loudon, Tennessee

Julius Ogden dismantled bombs during World War II. To loosen him up and lighten his meticulous and treacherous work, his fellow soldiers started calling him "Tic."

When he returned home to Loudon, Tennessee, Julius figured if he was steady enough to neutralize a bomb, he could go to town on a Bulova watch. So he secured a good corner location across from the Loudon County Courthouse and opened Tic-Toc Jewelers.

Couples would buy their wedding rings from Tic, and once they got settled in a house they'd return for a television set. They still come to that 110-year-old building today and talk about how their rings and marriages have lasted over the years, but now there's no diamond polishing or resizing, no class rings or brooches to buy.

The Tic-Toc is now an ice cream parlor. People around this Tennessee River community already call it an institution, even though it's only been open since 1999.

Tom Roberts scrapped his New York City advertising business and his wife Kimberly abandoned her Manhattan beauty salon to come south and sell ice cream, all homemade.

In the summer of 2005 they made a change nearly as radical. They sold the business and drove 4,000 miles through Central America to Costa Rica, where Tom now paints landscapes and Kimberly is learning the native cuisine. For the first three months they studied Spanish five and a half hours a day.

They have no worries about their East Tennessee ice cream business, though. It's in the hands of Bob and Mary Jones. This was no hostile takeover. It's as cordial a transition as you could imagine.

Bob retired from the paper industry in Louisiana and Mary left her job as a hospital human resources manager to join him in Loudon. They knew nothing about the ice cream business, but they've been tutored and patiently

Samantha Glass of Loudon and a cone of Chattanooga Chocolate. *Photo by Fred Sauceman.*

coached by Tom and Kimberly through the ins and outs of flavorings, freezing techniques, and syrup science.

"They've been great mentors," says Bob, who had purchased a retirement home nearby in Tellico Plains several years ago. He'd been looking for a business and found this one on the Internet.

"Unannounced, we came in right at noon and had a banana split. Kimberly waited on us, then Tom. We crossed the street and sat at the courthouse and saw people trickle in. We came back at 7 o'clock and sat on the corner like private detectives. Two cars came around the corner, parked, and all four doors opened. People went running in, and we couldn't believe it. We'd never seen anything like it."

Bob and Mary adhere to the "why mess with a good thing" philosophy. The butterfat content of the ice cream is going to stay at 14 percent. They'll keep making ice cream every day for five hours, 5 gallons at a time, in a horizontal homemade batch freezer.

They may extend the season, from early May on through until the middle of November, and they may throw in some new flavors they heard about at the Penn State Ice Cream Retailing Seminar, but that's about it as far as change goes.

At the Tic-Toc, ice cream is served in cones, it isn't mixed on cold rocks, and the sundaes come in glasses, not Styrofoam.

Kimberly says she learned to predict the flavor of ice cream a person will order based on age.

"Butter pecan's a mature flavor. People under thirty rarely order it."

The firecracker is a favorite among the youth league soccer set. It's bubble-gum pink, cotton-candy-flavored, and studded with exploding Pop Rocks.

The entire Tic-Toc menu is also posted on the wall in Spanish. Chocolate y Frambuesa, a chocolate-raspberry truffle flavor, is among the most popular of the ice creams.

Blackout is chocolate with chocolate chunks. Chattanooga Chocolate is plain chocolate—the name was chosen purely for the alliteration. There's no connection to the city down Interstate 75.

Come cooler weather, Bob and Mary freeze up batches of ice cream with flavors like pumpkin pie, chocolate hazelnut, and rum raisin.

The Tic-Toc keeps about eighteen ice creams on hand all the time, from simple strawberry to complex peanut butter crunch. They're stored in plastic barrels inside a Kelvinator freezer, with yellow sticky notes on the outside to mark the position of each flavor.

Your sundae's likely to be layered by a nurse doubling as a soda jerk, a dancer who's plied her trade in Israel, a cross-country runner, or a University of Mississippi graduate student. A recent Tic-Toc newsletter says, "We don't hire smokers nor people lacking a sense of humor."

The Jones and Roberts families come from markedly different backgrounds, but they've all learned to talk up the virtues of butterfat.

Says Bob, "I've got the physique of an ice cream maker."

The Tic-Toc Ice Cream Parlor
504 Grove Street
Loudon, Tennessee
(865) 408-9867

The Divine Secrets of Syrup and Sugar

At Christmastime the young women in Ada Hornsby Earnest's home economics classes at East Tennessee State College took home more than knowledge. For the train trip back home they packed away cartons of divinity candy, stirred and stiffly beaten by the hands of their experienced teacher, who claimed her foamy formula "never failed."

"No doubt her recipe has been used hundreds of times across the years by homemakers and home economics teachers throughout the East Tennessee area," recalls former student and later colleague Carsie Lodter of Johnson City, who kept the tradition of giving divinity to her own students.

Mrs. Earnest taught in one of the original departments, "Domestic Science," after having enrolled as a student in 1912, the very first year of East Tennessee State Normal School's existence. According to an early catalogue, the required course in home economics covered "the necessities of daily home life, the material and forces with which the housekeeper has to deal."

For Mrs. Earnest divinity candy was a way to add grandeur and elegance to those necessities, elevating the most accessible of ingredients—water, sugar, syrup, eggs, vanilla, and nuts—to a confection worthy of its churchly name.

The Joy of Cooking warns candy makers that divinity should only be made on a dry day. Kelly Ehlinger of Houston, Texas, says her father, a petroleum engineer, brings a meticulous level of precision and measured control to his candy-making.

"He checked the barometric pressure before starting the humidity-sensitive divinity when we were living on Corpus Christi Bay," she remembers. "At seventy-four, he continues to make divinity for our family at Christmas every year. His job required us to move all over the world and the States, but we could always count on a relative sending us some Texas pecans wherever we were, in time for candy-making. It was one of the special things he did that brought a 'sameness' and family tradition to wherever we were.

Ada Hornsby Earnest. *Photo courtesy East Tennessee State University.*

"He has certain pans he uses for the candy. When making Easter dinner, my mother might say, 'Let's put that in the divinity pan.'"

Gurniadean Myers kept the hen population of Morgantown, West Virginia, in business. If she wasn't bringing divinity to a church or community gathering, she brought custard or a meringue-crowned pie.

"That woman knew her eggs," says Janeen Bradford of Morgantown. "She was an active lady, manning election boards, attending every committee and woman's group at church, knowing the scoop on everyone from eight to eighty and often praying for their souls. Gurniadean has been gone to the big Methodist Women's Society meeting in the sky for many years, but the image of this 4-foot, 11-inch wizened little woman carrying a plate of divinity in one hand and Bible tracts in the other still lives in legend and lore up on this hill."

For Al "The Mayor" Bowen of Lanesville, Indiana, divinity evokes memories not of hearth and home but of life on the highway.

"We have always used divinity as the excuse for a stop at a Stuckey's whenever we travel. Especially on I-40 out West, those Indian tourist stops for gas and snacks do help break up the trip. The little puffs of divinity are so melt-in-your-mouth good, it's hard to control your intake.

"I know these are commercially-made, but the feeling of connecting to the trips we made across the country even back to the 1940s goes a lot deeper than the light chunks of candy. Tasting divinity at one of those odd-roofed huts brings back memories of things like the grandparents' dog that rode with me in a 1950 Studebaker and my honeymoon trip out West in 1963. When we stop today, we not only get snacks, we get a chance to peek into our personal family travel history."

Ada Hornsby Earnest, who died in 1982 at age ninety-six, used to recite the "Prayer of a Homemaker" to each one of her home economics classes at East Tennessee State. She did so for the final time in 1963, eight years after she had retired from teaching. The prayer speaks of the homemaker seeking sainthood not by quiet contemplation and study but through the dignity of work, "by getting meals and washing up the plates."

Folks around East Tennessee who have made her divinity recipe late in December for years without blemish, fault, or imperfection say her prayer was answered.

Mrs. Earnest's Never-Fail Divinity

1/3 cup water
1 1/3 cups white sugar
1/3 cup white Karo syrup
1 egg white, stiffly beaten
1 teaspoon vanilla
1/2 cup chopped nuts, coconut, or candied cherries.
(Mrs. Earnest used green and red cherries at Christmastime.
When she used nuts, it was usually pecans or black walnuts.)

Cook together the water, sugar, and Karo syrup until it spins a thread. (Some old candy thermometers have a marking for "Thread," at around 230 degrees. The "thread" is a very thin, wispy filament that appears when you dip a spoonful of the mixture out of the pan.) Pour half the syrup over the stiffly beaten egg white, beating all the time. Cook the remaining syrup to the "crack" stage (300 degrees) when tested in cold water. Continue beating the first mixture while pouring the rest of the syrup into it. When it begins to hold its shape, add vanilla and nuts, coconut, or cherries. Continue beating until it holds its shape well. If it should not hold its shape as desired, add a tablespoon of sifted powdered sugar, or 2 tablespoons, if needed. Drop from teaspoon onto waxed paper. Cool and store in airtight box.

Snapping Up Turtles and Winning Hearts in Sulphur Springs

They're teachers, businesswomen, housewives, and retirees. They're Methodists. And they're meticulous. Each winter, in the weeks before Valentine's Day, these United Methodist Women rush out of their homes, offices, and classrooms and converge in the kitchen at Sulphur Springs United Methodist Church in rural Washington County, Tennessee, where they lace on aprons and make turtles.

It's a good time for candy production. The church covered-dish dinner schedule's a little lighter with the passing of the holidays, and it's still eight months before parishioners barbecue 450 chicken halves for the Harvest Festival.

People around Sulphur Springs live by tradition, so it's likely the UMW's four years of immersion in chocolate and caramel will turn into decades. The Carders, the Squibbs, the Sherfeys, and the Deakinses have lived between these ridges for nearly two centuries. Wedged among encroaching brick ranch houses are cattle farms that have been in the same families since the 1820s.

In 2004 Sulphur Springs United Methodist held its 185th camp meeting. Beside the current church sits a metal-roofed shed, built in 1900 from many of the hand-hewn beams pastor William Milburn hauled out of the woods and lashed together for the original 1845 structure.

In its earliest days Sulphur Springs was part of a circuit, a collection of churches under the leadership of a single pastor. For nearly two decades now it has been a "station church," a congregation with its own minister.

"The congregation historically has shared a unique relationship with nearby Sulphur Springs Baptist Church," says former pastor Jonathan Jonas. "In previous generations, it was not at all uncommon for married couples to divide their participation and membership between the two. The husband might be a member of one, and the wife a member of the other.

Bobbie Carder makes chocolate-encased peanut-butter hearts, with help from Carolyn Maden.
Photo by Larry Smith.

"One leader in the congregation says he avoided listening to a sermon for years as a child by choosing which parent he accompanied to church. Since both congregations were circuit churches, they didn't have preaching every week, and he always attended whichever church wasn't having preaching that Sunday."

Behind the 1921 bricked, 400-member Methodist church is a Community Ministry Center, where the winter candy-making takes place. Scribbled on a marker board mounted on the white cinder-block wall is the recipe for 12-banana pudding and instructions to deep-fry catfish for four minutes. On one of the stainless steel countertops is a sheet of round-cornered, computer-generated labels, each reading "Pray for Peace" and ready to be centered on a cellophane bag of chocolate turtles or hearts.

"The money from this candy all goes to mission projects," says Bobbie Carder, who has taught fifth grade next door at Sulphur Springs Elementary School for thirty-seven years.

"We've purchased a telephone tree system that allows us to stay in contact with all our members. We've bought a house that will function as a help center and food pantry for the community. We've bought groceries for folks who are having a hard time. We've paid light bills."

Pastor Jonas says the ladies' peanut-butter-filled hearts have an impact not only locally but internationally.

"The candy sold here at Sulphur Springs has an effect on those recovering from the tsunami in Southeast Asia and supports mission work in East Africa."

For two and a half hours after school the church kitchen is filled with vats of melting chocolate. Practicing the patience that has come from years in elementary school classrooms, these United Methodist Women carefully spoon the hot chocolate into plastic turtle-shaped molds and drizzle in fat-free caramel that retains some of its liquidity after the candy sets. A pecan half is nested on top, the candy is cooled, and then the turtle is iced with more milk chocolate.

A blend of peanut butter, cream cheese, and butter forms the center of the hearts, which are encased in chocolate, and there's always a batch filled with coconut and butter.

For Valentine's Day the candy is bagged in cellophane with pink and red hearts and tied with wired red foil. It's all sold by word of mouth.

To these devoted ladies, Valentine's Day is more than Cupid and arrows. It's a time to express the caring and compassion of a community of faith going back 200 years, through the sweetness and joy of chocolate.

How Khrushchev Killed
Our Snow Cream

Growing up under the clouds of Cold War Communism affected us Baby Boomers in deep and lasting ways. The yellow-and-black fallout shelter insignias on our communities' most solid buildings, the elementary school drills that forced us under our desks in a severely constrained fetal position, and the frightening countenances on national television of the shoe-pounding Nikita Khrushchev and fiery Fidel Castro created a frightening world and a sense of impending doom for those of us who were forming our view of things in the late 1950s and early 1960s.

One of the most memorable Cold War losses in my own life was our snow cream, once we learned that nuclear warheads were being tested in the atmosphere and "fallout" became as regular a part of the lexicon as "hoola hoop."

Now, in the era after the Nuclear Test Ban Treaty, ozone depletion and environmental pollutants have supplanted paranoia over the Russians, but my mother has resumed making snow cream. She says even thinking about proportions is a silly proposition and that you should scoop up a bowlful of fresh snow, add sugar and vanilla flavoring to taste, mix in enough milk to get it the way you want it, and eat the results immediately, no matter who's in power at the time.

Vanilla Summers

The Virtues of Hand-Cranked Homemade Ice Cream

It was the longest stretch of time. Even the cranking job seemed to go quicker, tedious and tiring as it was. But when the frosty metal cylinder in the ice cream maker wouldn't turn any more and the kitchen towel was laid on top of the barrel so the ice cream could ripen, the wait was unending, almost unendurable. After all, fruit had to ripen, and that took weeks.

In the hour or so required for a freezer of homemade ice cream to solidify or cure, children like me would abandon their posts at first base or third, run to the adult who'd done most of the cranking, and ask, "Is it ready yet?" We interjected the question with the same persistence and frustration that emanated repeatedly from the back seats of station wagons on vacation: "How much farther is it?"

The old hand-cranked ice cream freezer was a shrine back then, the unifying element of summer afternoon backyard picnics. Being chosen to take your turn at the crank meant you'd made it, that the strength of your arm now commanded the respect of the elders. Some parents required a minimum number of cranks before you handed off the responsibility to someone else and headed back to the makeshift baseball diamond behind the house. Some children shortened their rite of passage, surreptitiously counting their turns by fives and tens.

In those days before the electric freezers took over, the tumbling of store-bought chunks of ice and the grinding and swishing of rock salt were among summer's most memorable sounds. We'd never heard of carpal tunnel syndrome, and we'd never admit to tennis elbow.

Our freezer was spring-green and barrel-like, with vertical staves held tight by rusting metal bands. It made the rounds of family reunions, church socials, Fourth of July picnics, and Sunday afternoon cookouts on the banks of chilly Horse Creek in Greene County, Tennessee.

There was never a question about the choice of flavor. Homemade ice cream meant vanilla. Period. No debate. Adding strawberries or peaches, much as we treasured them sugared in bowls by themselves, was out of the question. Even cake was unnecessary and frivolous ornamentation. To offer toppings of chocolate syrup, maraschino cherries, or nuts was sacrilege, as unthinkable as serving commercial ice cream at a birthday party.

Once that towel was whisked off the freezer with a flourish, once the paddle inside the cylinder had been scraped clean of ice cream, pandemonium ensued. Gloves were tossed off and left in the outfield. Children catapulted themselves out of swing sets in mid-arc.

There were no dietary cautions about eating ice cream made with real eggs then. Soft and arctic cold, tongue-tingling homemade ice cream was eaten with abandon. Children only stopped to recover from annoying but temporary brain-freeze headaches.

Nowadays, when ice cream can be produced with a few facile turns of a plastic-handled machine in an air-conditioned kitchen, turned out effortlessly by an electric freezer sitting abandoned on the patio, or purchased in shopping-mall ice cream boutiques, we miss the lessons those old hand-cranked machines taught so many generations during sweltering Southern summers—that those things coming to us the quickest and easiest aren't always the best. Those wooden, arm-powered ice cream freezers taught us patience, the virtue of waiting for what is good. They helped us realize that honest labor, shared with others, will eventually be rewarded. And oh what a reward it was.

Brianna Long assists her mother Melissa in making handcranked, homemade ice cream at the Blue Plum Festival, Johnson City, Tennessee. *Photo by Larry Smith.*

6

Loaf and Linger

We eat our way through Tennessee's oldest town,
pursue the elusive Banana Flip, entertain cats the color
of Scottish marmalade, and get down to Frog Level.

Touring Three of the Nation's Oldest Mills

St. John Milling Company, Watauga, Tennessee

Tennessee's oldest business survived flaming Yankee raids in 1862 and the coming of the discount stores a century later. A monument to the determination and perseverance of the mountain people who've kept it going for over 225 years, St. John Milling Company in Watauga, Tennessee, sits on the banks of north-flowing Brush Creek right on the Washington-Carter County line.

George St. John, now in his nineties, obtained the once decaying, out-of-date mill, applied his newly acquired engineering knowledge from the University of Tennessee, and began modernizing the business during the Depression. The 1900 census reported over forty mills in operation in Washington County. By mid-century most all of them were boarded up. Seeing a dim future in grinding corn and wheat, St. John and his son-in-law Ron Dawson bought equipment from some of those closed mills and created a farm store and feed mill. Ten years ago the bulk of their business was cattle feed, but today it's sweet feed for horses.

The earthy smell and creaky floors of the Southern feed store and the rush of the cool creek just outside the back door make St. John Mill one of East Tennessee's most beloved places. Farmers know they can come by and find a new T-post for fence-mending or a pulley for the barn. The store sells Grape Balm Hoof Healer, gopher bait, and apple-flavored horse treats. Along with each purchase comes the timeless wisdom of the feed store proprietor. Buy the Have-a-Heart trap and you learn the best way to catch raccoons—the folks at St. John were battling an unusually large population of the pesky animals one year when a customer suggested baiting the traps with marshmallows.

"The next morning, we had two 'coons in one trap," Ron says. More good advice: take a trip with the catch and transport the animals a minimum

George St. John's engineering knowledge saved this eighteenth-century mill in Watauga, Tennessee. *Photo by Larry Smith.*

of 7 miles from where they were caught. Make it only 6, Ron adds, and they'll revisit.

It's the age-old exchange of information and stories, opinions and predictions that has taken place around courthouse benches and country stores in these mountains ever since settlers got together in 1772 to organize the Watauga Association, America's first independent government. It wasn't long afterward that Jeremiah Dungan, chased off a British hunting preserve in Bucks County, Pennsylvania, found a small, falling stream with a 16-foot gradient that could be harnessed for milling. By 1778 he was in business on Brush Creek. Farmers shelled their corn by hand and brought their "turn" in cotton sacks.

"The miller dipped his toll box into the grain to get his share, usually about 7 or 8 pounds per bushel," says George. When fall harvest time came, settlers and their families camped outside the mill and talked politics with their neighbors until time to grind their wheat or corn.

With a book of deeds, letters, and tax records dating back to 1784, George, whose grandfather bought the mill in 1866, has become an amateur historian. He and Ron, who purchased the business from his father-in-law in 1975, have thought long and hard about how the mill made it through the Civil War, especially with the bullets and the flames of Carter's Raid the day before New Year's Eve, 1862. They believe the mill escaped the Yankee raiders' torches only because it was run by a Dunkard minister, who led Sunday services there.

"It's hard to conceive how this mill survived, being 500 yards from where Carter's Raid happened, and being an established mill grinding wheat and corn when soldiers from both sides were trying to cut supply lines for food and ammunition," Ron says. "The only theory we find plausible is that it was used as a House of the Lord and therefore spared."

Immediately after the Civil War, East Tennessee was considered the "bread basket of the South," says George. "While much of the South was torn up during the War, there was very little damage here, and the mill's customer base expanded." The Read House in Chattanooga, once an Army hospital during the Civil War, baked with cornmeal and flour from St. John Mill.

Today even St. John's competitors are customers, and they often pool their money to buy truckloads of goods for a better price break. When two of Ron's employees had to miss work because of illness, instead of turning to the want ads or temporary employment services Ron was aided by a competitor. Mike Galloway, of Galloway's Mill in Sullivan County, sent over one of his men to St. John for two days and would accept no pay.

"Thirty years ago, Galloway's had a building burn," Ron explained. "George St. John sent over a truck and

St. John Milling Company
3191 Watauga Road
Watauga, Tennessee
(423) 928-5841

men to help them get back on their feet, and they never forgot it. You don't see that in business today."

Ron believes the mill's owners have prospered by getting past the idea that the only reason for their existence is to make money.

"We're working to give service, to help others. We've arrived when you have a businessman come in and you see him loosen his tie. That action says I don't have to put up a front for anyone. I can be myself. I think it's the way the Good Lord wanted us to be."

White's Mill, Abingdon, Virginia

White's Mill survived the Yankees, too, and the termites. The bugs were a more permanent threat than the Federals to this once water-powered landmark near Abingdon, Virginia, but Thomas Moffatt and a Welsh shipwright had studied insect-resistant woods enough to know that yellow poplar was their best bet.

That choice was made almost 220 years ago. Today the mill still stands on the banks of Tool's Creek in Washington County.

Moffatt and his Welsh buddy knew something about flooding, too. They situated their fledgling business at exactly the right spot on the brook where they could get maximum water power and minimum overflow.

The mill was named for its second owner, Colonel James White, who purchased it in 1838. In 1922 it came into the hands of a family of capital "M" Millers, in one of those cases where a family's name drives its destiny. The Millers milled there until 1988.

The mill is now in the hands of the White's Mill Foundation, a nonprofit organization campaigning to raise $600,000 for the restoration of water-powered grinding. James Miller, whose grandfather Scott made the 1922 purchase, runs the operation today.

"It's in pretty good shape for being built in the first year of George Washington's presidency," says James between entertaining a tour bus and restocking his supply of white cornmeal. "Federal troops tried to burn the mill down during the Civil War, but the fire was put out. They did blow out

White's Mill, Abingdon, Virginia. Photo by Fred Sauceman.

the dam up the valley, though. Afterward, there was an agreement that corn and wheat would be ground for both sides. That's how the mill survived."

The 22-foot overshot waterwheel stands quiet, but inside James grinds grain on a 1915-model Williams mill.

"I've been a miller all my life," he jokes.

Both white grits and yellow grits are ground on a granite buhrstone that was shipped over from France when the mill first opened for business in 1790. Corn is poured into a hopper to the center of the stone. The top stone, James explains, is a runner stone and the bottom, termed the bed stone, is grooved. As the corn works its way toward the outer casing, it is ground finer.

"There's a difference between a corn stone and a wheat stone," James instructs. Wheat for flour is ground in an 1894 roller mill at the rate of anywhere from 15 to 25 bushels an hour.

White cornmeal, white grits, whole-wheat flour, rye flour, buckwheat flour for pancakes, yellow cornmeal, yellow grits, and popcorn meal are sold at the mill itself or across the street in the mercantile store, where local crafts are also featured.

"The popcorn meal is used for cornbread and hush puppies," says James. "Popcorn has a sweeter taste. Back in the Civil War, grain was confiscated and all people had left was popcorn, the outer hull. Animals couldn't chew it, so it was ground into cornmeal."

Smithsonian Magazine, in its October 1999 issue, makes the case for grits as America's first food, as evidenced by the Powhatan Indians serving cracked maize porridge to the country's first European settlers. That assertion was later cited by the Georgia General Assembly in a bill designating grits as the "official prepared food" of the state.

Whether eaten as homage to history, foil for Georgia chauvinism, or an excuse to consume gobs of butter, White's Mill grits, stone-ground and evocative of the scent of the cornfield, is good—to use the singular verb preferred by many Southern grits grammarians.

White's Mill
White's Mill Road, located about
4 1/2 miles outside Abingdon,
Virginia, on Route 692
(276) 628-2960

Falls Mill, Belvidere, Tennessee

The waters of Factory Creek, captured and diverted through a millrace, rush over the top of the 32-foot steel waterwheel at Falls Mill near Belvidere in lower Middle Tennessee. Each month about 18,000 pounds of corn and wheat pass through the 42-inch granite buhrstones, which date back to

William Janey bags up grits at Falls Mill, Belvidere, Tennessee. *Photo by Larry Smith.*

1900. The mill itself was constructed out of brick and poplar in 1873 and was first used as a textile factory for spinning yarn and making cloth.

Jane Lovett, an anthropologist who, in a previous life, taught sign language to orangutans, bought the property in 1984 along with her husband John, who once taught engineering students.

At least 65 percent of the Lovetts' business consists of grits, ground from corn grown by area farmers. In addition to the appurtenances of the miller's craft, the Lovetts own and exhibit "the ultimate kitchen gadget of the 1880s," a butter churn powered by a dog running on a treadmill.

William Janey, the man who works the buhrstones, is a proud consumer of his product. "I still turkey-hunt, and the camp cook will boil grits with a little bacon grease, salt, and pepper," the miller tells visitors. "Whatever's left over makes a great grits casserole."

About 20,000 visitors come through the mill every year, many of them toting picnic baskets.

"My husband first came to Falls Mill on picnics with old girlfriends," says Jane. "Our mill is powered by the waters of Factory Creek, which is spring-fed and runs year-round. The waterwheel will soon be 100 years old. There are fewer than 150 water-powered mills still operating commercially in this country. At one point there were fifty in Franklin County alone. One of our biggest challenges is flooding. The stairs down to the water level were built after the Christmas flood of 1990. We had 14 inches of rain in thirty-six hours during that flood. The water rose so high that if you were standing on the top stair, you would have been 3 feet under water.

"Our specialty item is slow-cooking, old-fashioned grits. A lot of restaurants in the coastal Carolinas serve them. We have a distributor out in Vancouver, Washington. And our best known accounts in Tennessee are Blackberry Farm and the Loveless Café at the northern terminus of the Natchez Trace Parkway near Nashville. I prefer savory grits, simmered for about twenty minutes in two parts chicken stock to one part grits. Sometimes I put in some minced onion or a little garlic and stir in some cream and cheese."

Falls Mill, an airy, three-story structure, is listed on the National Register of Historic Places. Painted on a rock inside the door of the mill is the admonition "Save the planet. It's the only one with cornbread."

Falls Mill and Country Store
134 Falls Mill Road
Belvidere, Tennessee
(931) 469-7161

Falls Mill Garlic Cheese Grits Casserole

1 cup stone-ground grits
2 cups water or chicken broth
1/4 teaspoon salt
1/4 teaspoon pepper
1/2 cup chopped onion
1/2 cup milk
1 egg
1 6-ounce roll garlic cheese
1 tablespoon butter

Place the grits in a bowl and cover with water. Stir. Skim off the chaff that rises to the top. Stir and skim again. Drain well. Bring 2 cups of water or broth to a boil in a saucepan. Stir in grits, salt, pepper, and chopped onion. Reduce heat to low and cook covered for thirty minutes, stirring occasionally, until grits are thick and creamy. Remove from heat. Combine milk and egg with the hot grits mixture using a wire whisk. Add cheese and butter; stir well. Spoon into a 1 1/2-quart baking dish coated with cooking spray. Bake at 375 degrees for forty minutes or until set. Makes six servings.

Christmas in Tennessee's Oldest Town

Scottish Cranachan and a Boone's Farm Punch

Scottish Magic at Poplar Hill

In the dining room at Poplar Hill, their 155-year-old home, Sam and Helen Thatcher drape ribbons of burgundy and green from the chandelier to the corners of the table. It's a practice dating back to the Victorian age, when many American and British Christmas traditions originated. Queen Victoria had been on the throne only thirteen years when the brick-and-wood home the Thatchers now occupy was built. The wings and bays projecting at unpredictable angles place the cross-shaped structure firmly within the Victorian architectural style. Its location, however, is far from the lands Victoria ruled for sixty-four years.

The Thatchers live in Tennessee's oldest town, Jonesborough, and their Christmas celebrations combine Sam's childhood traditions from Chattanooga and Helen's from a rural community 10 miles south of Edinburgh, Scotland. Their preparations for the holidays illustrate a common theme in this town of 4,300: veneration for the past.

Accomplished gardeners, the Thatchers use natural greenery throughout their home—evergreens, holly, ivy, and mistletoe. When family and friends visit for holiday meals, the house is illuminated only by candlelight.

"Each year we add some new decorations, usually for the tree, that we find if we are away somewhere," Helen says. "Our tree is a memory of all these places, tying them together, and of ornaments given over the years to us. It is quite a cluttered tree, not a designer one at all."

Helen's Christmas preparations differ in one respect from her parents'. She remembers going to bed on Christmas Eve as a girl in Scotland with the house completely undecorated. Her mother and father stayed up all night to create a Christmas wonderland, just in time for the opening of presents on Christmas morning. The meal was timed so that it wouldn't conflict with Queen Elizabeth's 3 P.M. Christmas radio address.

Jonesborough's Green Mansion, built in 1825. *Photo by Peter Montanti, Mountain Photographics, Inc.*

As a reproductive endocrinologist, Dr. Sam Thatcher has brought into the world hundreds of children, many to couples who had previously given up hope of becoming parents. Yet the Thatchers themselves have no children. Their home is populated by a lively Airedale terrier, with the Celtic name of Eilidh, and six cats, two of whom are the golden color of Scottish marmalade. One of them, 20-pound Ruaraidh, can leap easily from floor to dining room table.

Eilidh and the cats all wear bows on Christmas, and each is given a filled stocking. Stockings are hung at the foot of each bed as well. "Although grown, we still do leave a wee something for Santa," Helen says. "We still believe in the magical."

On a candlelit Yuletide, the Thatchers flame a hearty and dark Christmas pudding moistened with brandy and brandy butter. Inside is a coin, wrapped in grease-proof paper, to bring the finder good luck.

Turkeys alternate with geese on the Christmas table, each baked in an oven named Daisy. Sam and Helen were roaming through a salvage store in Marietta, Georgia, when they witnessed the arrival of a 1920s-vintage stove. The proprietor told them he hadn't initially intended to sell it because it was purchased for the film *Driving Miss Daisy*. With two extra eyes on the left-hand side, however, the stove was too big for the movie set. Sam and Helen bought it, and it is their sole means of cooking.

"For goose, judging the amount can be horrific," Helen says. "We always take extra poundage because of the amount of fat in the bird."

Family members are seated at 2 P.M. on Christmas day and each is required to open a cracker—not the edible kind but rather a cardboard tube with a snap that's pulled to release small gifts, a joke on a slip of paper, and a hat to be worn after the first course, with Helen's insistence.

The past is very much present at the Thatchers' holiday table. A nineteenth-century mural, updated and personalized by Barbara Ferrell in the 1990s, covers an entire dining room wall. Sam's childhood Airedale roams the painted fields amid grazing sheep, remembrances of the Scottish hills where Helen played as a girl.

Every December, Helen relives the year when the snow came on Christmas Eve. "Family were here for the holidays. It was quite magical, with the candles and fire roaring in the fireplaces and all the festive greens and the tree smelling so wonderfully fresh of the outdoors. We made snowmen in the garden."

The Fragrance of Cedar on Main

For Sue and Gerald Henley, twenty-year residents of a former tailor shop on Main Street in Jonesborough, Tennessee, Christmas means cedar. "I love to use it because it reminds me of my dad," Sue remembers. "We always cut a cedar tree each year. It just smells like Christmas to me."

The wooden Santas and felt ornaments on the Henleys' cedar Christmas tree go back three decades. Raggedy Ann and Andy, an Amish couple, and a black poodle that makes Sue think of a beloved family dog from the 1970s swing from cedar boughs.

"Spending Christmas in Jonesborough is wonderful because it's more calm and traditional," Sue says. "You can shop without the hassle of long lines. Just walking up the street is a pleasure. The decorations are beautiful and festive."

The Henleys' 1840 Federal-style brick home sits right on Main Street a few paces from the "upping block," a stepped, stone structure once used for boarding horse-drawn carriages. With candles glowing through frost-covered windows flanked by the home's original wooden shutters, the Naff-Henley House is one of the town's most visible signs of Christmas.

The Henleys and a close circle of friends meet every year in early December for breakfast at the Cranberry Thistle to make out the menu for their annual potluck dinner, held at the Henley House a week before the holiday. Like any good Southern potluck gathering, it's a mixture of the new and the traditional. On Gerald's grandfather's old oak table, Mayor Tobie Bledsoe always serves her Greek salad. Sherry Harrison wouldn't be invited in without bringing a bowl of homemade salsa. Town administrator Bob Browning brings ribs and chicken. And Hal Knight's banana pudding, topped with a lightly browned meringue, is described by Sue as "a work of art." Ham, seafood, a soufflé of sweet potatoes, and a mayonnaise-based potato salad with fresh cucumbers and tomatoes are always on the assignment sheet along with Sue's Festive Punch, a favorite of her late grandfather George Payne, a banjo player who made moonshine as a youth in Greene County.

Every room in the house is decorated. The Christmas tree and the mantle in the parlor carry a Victorian theme. Gold, crystal, and mauve color the family room, and the kitchen, with a linen chest from the 1820s and a pie safe that is original to the house, is decorated in a country style. Below the Blue Willow china on the mantle, the fireplace still shows century-old scars where matches were struck when it was the room's only source of heat for warming bodies and roasting game.

Once the potluck dishes are cleared, Sue begins preparations for her family's Christmas dinner, always served in the evening. She selects a real country ham, scrubs it, soaks it for three days with frequent water changes, and bakes it. A standard accompaniment is three-bean salad, in memory of her grandmother, who always requested that dish for the holiday table. A moist and spicy Tennessee blackberry jam cake ends the meal.

Sue Henley's Festive Punch

2 bottles Boone's Farm Apple Wine
1/2 pint apricot brandy
1 quart apple juice

Mix ingredients, chill, and serve.

Dining Progressively

During the first weekend in December, visitors from throughout the region are carried around town on trolley cars for the annual Progressive Dinner, a project of the Jonesborough-Washington County Heritage Alliance.

The Progressive Dinner is part history lesson, part concert, part architectural tour, and primarily a feast. The night begins with an English wassail toast, then it's on to a series of homes, such as the 1793 Hawley House on Jonesborough's Lot Number One where guests were once served a creamy shrimp bisque chosen by owner Marcy Hawley, a native of Charleston, South Carolina. Diners from years past recall the flaming plum pudding with the Kennedy family, sweet potato pecan pie with the Henleys, and smoked ham with the Bledsoes.

At the former location of Baptist institutes for females and males, a Civil War hospital for Union and Confederate troops, and a school for freed slaves run by Quakers, Gary and Alexis Burkett have served key lime pie.

Some years diners gather for dessert around the wood stove at the old Oak Hill School while the Jonesborough Novelty Band plays Christmas carols on banjo and guitar. Relocated from the Knob Creek Community in Washington County, the school hosts area children by day, using a curriculum taught according to the styles and subjects of 1892.

Hallways of homes are filled with vocalists, harpists, string duets, pianists, and flutists performing Christmas carols from around the world. For some, the music rivals the cuisine.

"The food at the Progressive Dinners is outstanding," writes Washington County sessions judge John Kiener. "But the bonus for me is the music. I was thrilled to discover there was musical entertainment at each dinner location."

The Heritage Alliance recruits fifty volunteers from the community each year to run the dinner. They plate the food, bring it to the diners, and hurriedly clean and reset the tables before the next group arrives. A local chiropractor transports provisions from a central cooking location to each home. A circuit of cellular phone calls keeps hosts apprised of exact arrival times so the chaotic and often frantic preparation will be totally unnoticed once guests ring doorbells. In two evenings, 270 people are fed and entertained at four locations. The volunteers throw a late-night party with leftovers before deciding how they themselves will celebrate Christmas with family and friends in a few days according to the time-honored customs of Jonesborough.

Helen Thatcher's Scottish Cranachan

A "Touch of Scotland" was served by Helen and Sam Thatcher for the fifteenth annual Jonesborough Progressive Dinner in 1992.

This traditional Scottish dessert is sometimes called "crowdie cream" by many Scots, since a soft cheese of that name was used in place of the cream.

1/2 cup pinhead or coarse oatmeal
1/2 pint of double cream
1 tablespoon Drambuie liqueur or a few drops of vanilla extract

Toast the oatmeal in a frying pan on high heat until lightly brown. Whisk the cream into a soft consistency and mix in the oatmeal and Drambuie or vanilla. Serve in tall glasses. A popular variation is to mix in 1 1/2 cups of fresh raspberries. Vanilla ice cream can also be used instead of cream.

A Storyteller's Hangout

Main Street Café, Jonesborough, Tennessee

On the first weekend of October during the National Storytelling Festival you may hear some outlandish tales under the tents in Jonesborough, Tennessee—but believe it when someone directs you to a place that serves a quarter-pound hot dog.

When it comes to the bun-busting Main Street Dog at Main Street Café, I take a conservative approach to condiments: brown mustard and either kraut or relish, a choice driven by the contents of the dessert case. It's a yin-yang balance. A forthcoming ultra-sweet dessert means sauerkraut on the dog.

Everything at Main Street is relative. Whether you choose a reasonably sized cream cheese almond bar or a robust piece of Kahlúa silk pie is dictated by your initial decision about a cup versus a bowl of soup.

Owners Herman and Beverly Jenkins are pushed regularly by sales reps trying to sell them pre-prepared soups. For twenty-five years they've resisted, and there are no plans to relent.

I can't ever remember eating at Main Street without having soup. Homemade soup selections are written on the chalkboard six days a week. Famous Potato Soup has a chicken broth base and is seasoned with yellow onion and garlic. Cheese and bacon elevate it to Loaded Potato Soup status.

"When I think about Main Street, I think about the people who own it and how they have supported the community so strongly," says storyteller Donald Davis of Ocracoke Island, North Carolina. "The magical thing about the place is the people."

Davis's signed photograph, along with a few dozen other raconteurs, hangs on one of the restaurant's lemon-colored walls to form a makeshift storytelling hall of fame.

The 1930s-era structure housing Main Street Café was built to government specifications as a United States post office. Its 14-foot ceilings are

The quarter-pound Main Street Dog. *Photo by Fred Sauceman.*

covered with original pressed tin. Sun streams in through tall, wide windows and blends with light from hanging globe lamps.

Evident in the way they dressed up the old post office, Herman and Beverly are masters at altering the commonplace just enough so that it's still recognizable but at the same time refreshingly different. The typical mayonnaise-based tuna salad "you grew up with," as Beverly puts it, is transformed into Mediterranean Tuna Salad with kalamata olives, artichoke hearts, marinated red peppers, thinly sliced purple onion, and a lemon-oregano vinaigrette dressing. Herbs are common on the Main Street menu, and they're harvested from the Jenkins' backyard garden.

"What have you done to this Reuben sandwich?" is a question servers hear often. Beverly's usually glad to share a recipe, but what she adds to

Thousand Island dressing for brighter color and more tartness is a business secret.

For her carrot-ginger cake she soaks long, thin strips of carrot in sugar water then drapes them over the cake like glistening orange ribbons. It's not unusual to see over twenty desserts in the glass case at one time—sweets like spring-green mint brownies and pastel-colored ambrosia cake.

The Jenkinses are one of Jonesborough's hardest-working families. Children Breelyn and Zachary grew up in the restaurant business. Both have sandwiches named after them. About 80 percent of the family's weekends are filled with weddings, rehearsal dinners, graduation soirées, and anniversaries. Exclusive "753 parties," with the title taken from the local telephone exchange, involve Jonesborough residents only, but people come from throughout the Tri-Cities for catering assistance administered out of the 1890s-era Old Quarters just up the street from the restaurant.

Beverly remembers Dallas-sized barbecues and big parties from her childhood, so numbers don't intimidate her. She estimates catering about 150 events a year. Guests at wedding receptions enjoy such colorful dishes as Chicken Cakes with Cilantro Lime Mayonnaise and Mango Garnish, or even Hollywood Boneless Ribs, which, as Beverly notes on "Elegant Menu Three," are "not messy at all."

Sitting at Main Street's wooden tables and booths you'll encounter folks in Birkenstocks and business suits and a good blend of tourists and locals. Whether you're a visitor for the Storytelling Festival in the fall or a home-towner taking care of a little business at the courthouse nearby, the hospitality, kindness, and culinary talent of the Main Street staff make a visit to this eighteenth-century neighborhood a pleasure in any season.

Main Street Café and Catering
117 West Main Street
Jonesborough, Tennessee
(423) 753-2460

A Four-Course Street Meal

Wallace News, Kingsport, Tennessee

I've always appreciated newsstands. During my reporting days at WKPT-TV in Kingsport, Tennessee, when there'd be a lull in police radio traffic and our stories had been filed for the day, we'd amble off to one of several such purveyors of knowledge and nourishment. Jimmy John's was a close walk. We called it Immy Ohn's because both Js had dropped off the back door.

The consummate, the archetype, the pinnacle and prototype of all newsstands will always be, for me, Wallace News on Broad Street. In the warm months it's open-air. You can walk in right off the street and never twist a doorknob. Drawn in by the smell of freshly popped popcorn, folks invariably slow down once they enter Wallace News. It's a place where sauntering and loafing are respected and encouraged.

When Kingsport attorney Burkett McInturff started having leg trouble and getting out of his car became difficult, Marty Mullins and Troy Brown began carrying the morning's *Times-News* and *Knoxville News-Sentinel* to him as his auto idled out on Broad.

"Wallace News is a great asset to Kingsport," said the longtime lawyer, whose office is just up the street. "I have a high regard for the people who work there. They are competent and honest, and they do a good job for the public."

Marty and Troy don't just sell newspapers, they study them. Recently I overheard Troy clarifying a headline on Eastman Chemical Company employment for a concerned customer. They can tell you the exact location of every magazine in the store—*Women's Day, Tattoos for Men, Quilting, Street Rodder, Texas Hunting, Bon Appetit, Mad,* and publications to suit every taste in between.

Each day the region's newspapers, gently blown by ceiling fans, are stacked on top of an old drink cooler.

Troy Brown oils up the popcorn at Wallace News. *Photo by Larry Smith.*

Wallace News is a business without a Web page or a computer work station, yet you feel connected to the world within its walls. You can purchase *The New York Times* every day, not just on Sundays.

The business opened in 1932 as Broad Street Fruit and News. Greenevillian Wallace Crum bought the newsstand in 1942 and operated it for thirty-two years before selling it to current owner Marty Mullins.

The popcorn machine is a converted hot dog cart that once rolled down the sidewalks of the Highland area in Kingsport throughout the 1940s. Crum sawed a hole in the bottom, rigged up a natural gas feed, and dropped in a stainless-steel popper for corn.

Marty credits much of the popcorn's memorable flavor to the popper—that and the cottonseed oil and seasoning blend, along with the absence of butter.

"Popcorn is a healthy food," Marty says.

Unless you saw someone on a Broad Street bench in mid-bite, you'd have virtually no way of knowing the newsstand sells hot dogs. They're reserved in Styrofoam containers in a refrigerator. Marty says keeping hot dogs under heat all day draws out the flavor. A quick dressing of chili imported from Knoxville, a squirt of mustard, a scattering of onions, a one-minute whirl in the microwave and your all-beef frank is ready to take to the street, along with one of the best cold drinks imaginable.

In 1968, says Troy Brown, Wallace News started dispensing frozen Pepsi-Cola products, which have become the heart of the business. The frozen Pepsi and frozen Mountain Dew are less airy and gassy than comparable products on the market. The syrup is expensive, Marty says, but the drink is superlative refreshment, one of the most satisfying cold beverages on the planet. Sometimes, if the consistency and temperature are just right, you can drink one without ever moving your straw.

For dessert Wallace stocks the elusive Kern's Bakery Banana Flip, a spongy cake folded into a half-circle with a light-yellow, flavored filling in between. Children who appeared on live late-afternoon television shows aired by Tri-Cities stations in the 1960s, before the age of sugar phobia, were often given Banana Flips as snacks.

With a hot dog, popcorn, frozen Pepsi, and Banana Flip from Wallace News, you've got a four-course street meal second to none.

Back inside, mint snuff, fried pork rinds, imported cigars, Black Toasted Cavendish pipe tobacco, crossword puzzle books, Louis L'Amour novels, and

Dr. Grabow pre-smoked pipes are all there for the browsing beneath life-size posters of Marilyn Monroe, James Dean, the Lone Ranger and Tonto, and a gallery of cowboys.

"People come in for the atmosphere and walk all the way through the store," says Marty.

Most stop awhile, though, knowing they've found a quiet place where they can return, even if only for a very few minutes, to the pace of the past.

Wallace News
205 Broad Street
Kingsport, Tennessee
(423) 245-2035

Chasing Pink Cloud Salads with Blackberry Milkshakes

Teddy's, Nickelsville, Virginia

You could call it an ice cream parlor. You could call it a short-order stop. You could call it an old-style Sunday family dinner restaurant. Folks in Nickelsville, Virginia, call it Teddy's. And whether you have a bear's appetite or just stop by for a baby cone of ice cream, it's a Highway 71 haven of good cooking.

Unpretentious owner Teddy Kilgore would just as soon you call it the Nickelsville Restaurant. It was the official name of a previous place he and his wife Trish used to run, but people insisted on calling it Teddy's. He figured since the name was so familiar to people, so easy to say and remember, he'd just use it when the current restaurant opened in 1986.

While Teddy is across the Virginia-Tennessee state line in Kingsport working as a chemical operator at Eastman, Trish is overseeing this twenty-year-old business that sits alongside Nickelsville's nerve center—the town hall, the water treatment plant, the fire department, and the rescue squad.

"This is the kind of place where working people take their daily meals," says Fire Chief Roger Burke, as he climbs over the red engine next door with a washrag and bucket. "They're swamped for Sunday dinner after church."

Chief Burke's been patronizing the same spot since he polished off cones of custard at the Dari-Kreme when he was a child. Trish Kilgore once bought 25-cent hamburgers there. She'd come down to Nickelsville on summer vacations from her home in Roda, a Wise County coal camp. Teddy and Trish's grandparents owned adjoining farms in Scott County, and that's how they met, over the fence.

Trish describes Teddy's hamburgers as "the backbone of the business." But they aren't billfold-breakers. A jumbo cheeseburger will cost you well under three dollars. Just to give you an idea of the size of the burger, two large slices of onion are placed side by side on the meat, and they don't overlap. These are burgers formed of finely ground, hand-patted chuck.

Trish Kilgore (left) with the Boyd sisters of Dungannon, Virginia, Crystal (center) and Cassie, servers at Teddy's. *Photo by Fred Sauceman.*

Their edges are irregular with bulges, pleats, and furrows, just like home-grilled.

In the mornings, as tenderloin fries and biscuits bake, hot dog chili simmers slowly on the stove for about two hours. This chili is mainly meat, with onions, seasonings, and very little sauce. My tasting notes read: "Spicy, chunky, meaty, and moist."

"The less liquid, the better, so the hot dog won't sog up," says Trish. "And did you ever eat a hot dog and the onions are going everywhere? We've solved that, when we make a slaw dog, by putting the onions on the bun, underneath the meat."

Teddy's serves a dye-less dog, on an Earth Grain bun. When I ordered a slaw dog at Teddy's, I didn't specify the condiments. I tend to avoid "special orders," preferring, instead, to experience a dish just like the restaurant normally prepares it. At Teddy's, that means mayonnaise on a slaw dog.

"I prefer mustard, but most people eat mayonnaise on their hot dogs around here," says Trish.

The restaurant's red and white curtains sport images of hamburgers and hot dogs.

For the Sunday feasts, Trish and the staff say there's no set menu. They cook whatever they feel like. Maybe turkey, dressing, and gravy. Or meatloaf. Or pepper steak, a mix of ground chuck, green peppers, eggs, and Worcestershire sauce. They're fried on the grill and then smothered in brown gravy. Pea salad, potato salad with mayonnaise and mustard, and cornbread salad are regular Sunday sides.

"It's like a big dinner for the family on Sunday," says Trish.

For dessert, Trish says the cooks at Teddy's can prepare a banana pudding with custard, but most customers go for the version that combines sour cream, whipped cream, and instant vanilla pudding. Strawberry jello, pineapples, other fruit, and cottage cheese coalesce as Pink Cloud Salad. The late June Carter Cash liked it so much, she asked for the recipe.

An English visitor came to Teddy's to eat one time, after he learned that Teddy's mother Faye is related to country music's Carter family.

"People come here regularly from Abingdon, Coeburn, Wise, Kingsport, and Gate City," says Teddy.

The dining area at Teddy's isn't segmented. It's all one big room, where you can admire and envy what everyone else orders—from dishes you'd expect, like hot fudge cake, to surprises like blackberry milkshakes.

Teddy's
Highway 71
Nickelsville, Virginia
(276) 479-3128

Souped-Up Bluegrass at Ciderville

Ciderville Music Store, Powell, Tennessee

On Wednesdays Faye West props her doghouse bass fiddle in the corner at the Ciderville Music Store and starts cutting up vegetables—celery, onions, and potatoes. The next morning she'll dice some tomatoes; add some butterbeans and mixed vegetables; sprinkle in some parsley, oregano, basil, and dried red pepper; drop in some bouillon cubes, a little bit of butter, a scattering of sugar, and some salt; and simmer it all down to make two big pots of vermilion vegetable soup that bring the bluegrass musicians out of the hills and hollows.

"I just come up with a combination that tasted good, that I liked, and I figured if I liked it, everybody else would, too."

At lunchtime every Thursday, Faye and her brother David serve soup free of charge to anyone who walks in the door. They'll set a few 2-liter softdrink bottles on the tables in the backroom kitchen, and Cecil Thomas will drive up from Lenoir City with his guitar in one hand and a pan of cornbread in the other. Pillars of saltines are unwrapped and stacked on the tables for the taking. No money ever changes hands.

"I've took the store out of the yellow pages, I've cut the newspaper ads," says David, who is one of the world's leading sellers of Martin guitars. "This is doing more for me than I ever got off of billboards or anything. It's just word of mouth, and there's probably going to be a hundred people here today."

David patterns his promotional tactics after longtime grocer and radio-and-television personality Cas Walker, whom he credits with the "invention" of the foot-long hot dog. He played banjo for Walker's broadcasts and owns the original television backdrop painted in 1958 by O. D. Abston. It was captured in black-and-white television camera shots of Dolly Parton, Don Gibson, and the Osborne Brothers and now frames the stage in a music hall behind the store, where Grand Ole Opry-style performances are held every Saturday night.

A Thursday afternoon jam session, after soup, at Ciderville. *Photo by Fred Sauceman.*

David witnessed Walker's outlandish promotional tactic of throwing live chickens off the roofs of his stores, and when Walker was nearing ninety David suggested he reconsider climbing on top of store roofs.

"We had this guy come out to Ciderville with one of these big cranes to lift us up on a big platform, and we threw paper fold-out turkeys to the customers down below. People would catch them and the turkeys would have a note on them saying you'd won a frozen turkey or guitar strings or a Cas Walker cap. Everybody won; every turkey had a prize on it.

"They called me from the Knoxville Humane Society and said that was cruelty to animals, and I said, 'Cruelty to animals? What are you gonna cook for Thanksgiving? How much worse can you get than to kill one, pluck it, cut it open, and bake it and then eat it?'"

Jam sessions break out all over the Ciderville Music Store, a starred and striped structure on the Clinton Highway about a mile inside the Anderson County line. Ten musicians mesh on the gospel tune "He Had to Reach Way Down for Me" while in the next room David West imitates clucking chickens on his banjo.

The West family used to press apples into cider on the spot where the music store now stands. Claude West started selling light groceries there in 1966. He and his children made the blocks for the building themselves.

Now the Wests sell guitars priced from a few hundred dollars to $50,000. "We sold Willie Nelson's family about ten just recently," says David.

Photographs of early country music personalities, mostly friends of the West family, are pinned to the walls all over the building. In the kitchen hangs a poster promoting Bonnie Lou and Buster, stars of *The Jim Walter Jubilee*, who gave David his start. He went to work for Cas Walker in 1976 and stayed until Walker's television show went off the air in 1984.

"It was a good bunch of people to work for. Nobody ever disagreed. Nobody tried to out-pick nobody. And Cas loved banjo picking, so if you played the banjo, you'd automatically get a job with Cas.

"I remember one time we had three television stations here in Knoxville, and at 7 o'clock in the morning he bought time on all three and put on a show sponsored by Cas Walker. He'd say, 'If you don't like what you're looking at, turn your channel,' and when you turned it, there's Cas Walker again. He'd say it on every one of them. He had it nailed down, didn't he?"

Like in the days of live television in East Tennessee, the banjo breakdowns, mandolin riffs, and guitar runs ring out from noon to 6 P.M. every Thursday at Ciderville Music Store—but by 1 the soup pot's usually dry and the cornbread's just crumbs.

Ciderville Music Store
2836 Clinton Highway
Powell, Tennessee
(865) 945-3595

No Yacht, No Gasoline

The Frog Level Service Station, Tazewell, Virginia

Whether you claim one of the six stools at T. E. Bowling's bar for a Diet Coke or a Yuengling from the oldest brewery in America, you're on hallowed ground near the Southwest Virginia town of Tazewell.

Like his father before him, T. E., Jr., runs the only gas station in the state where on-premises beer consumption is entirely legal despite the total absence of a kitchen.

"My father said beer isn't made to drink; it's made to sell," says the octogenarian bartender at the Frog Level Service Station, which opened at the nadir of the Great Depression in 1932.

"My father lived to be eighty-seven years old and said those days will come again, I'm afraid, and looking down the road right now, it kind of seems that way to me," he philosophizes.

T. E., Jr., stopped selling gasoline along about 1996, so other than some dried beef, dusty cans of Bluebird grapefruit juice, long-neglected pork and beans, and Vienna sausages for creek bank picnics, liquid refreshment is about all you'll find at Frog Level today—and T-shirts. Some 40,000 of them have gone out the door of this secluded tavern at a quiet mountain crossroads.

After Dr. Puck Kiser and his wife stretched one over the neck of a British scientist at the South Pole in 2001, the image of a green frog perched on a bar stool, clad in nautical headgear, and gripping a beer made it to every continent.

Buy a T-shirt or blazer and you're instantly installed as a member of the Frog Level Yacht Club. There's a fruit jar beside the cash register if you'd like to donate some coins toward the purchase of the yacht. Where the boat would float is anybody's guess, seeing as how Plum Creek's a bit too narrow for conventional yacht clearance.

The fog that wafts above Plum Creek on humid nights is the origin of this flyspeck hamlet's name. The late Jack Witten, principal of North

T. E. Bowling, Jr. *Photo by Fred Sauceman.*

Tazewell Elementary School for forty-three years, was fishing for redeye one summer night with a farmhand friend when a big fog rolled in.

"The frogs were hollering, and the story goes that the farmhand said the fog was so low, it was down to frog level, and the name stuck," says T. E. "Jack later called his newspaper column 'The Frog Level News.'"

When Prohibition was repealed in 1933, T. E. Bowling, Sr., applied for a beer license for his store, and it was Jack Witten who convinced him to name it the Frog Level Service Station. Witten also lobbied state senators and representatives to post a Frog Level sign, appropriately green, along the roadside.

Upon Bowling, Sr.'s death the beer license was "grandfathered" over to his son, and the business outlasted all competitors for the right to be Virginia's only bar with gasoline pumps.

"We've got lawyers, some doctors, farmers, coal miners, all walks of life come in here," says T. E., Jr. "We've got the rednecks over there and the college kids over here, and directly they'll get to mixing and mingling and you can't tell which side is which, and everybody gets along beautifully."

T. E. has assembled quite a collection of amphibiana—frogs carved out of Southwest Virginia coal and a clock that marks the changing of the hour with the chirping of a frog. On the tip of the second hand sits a plastic fly.

All manner of wisdom is bandied across this old bar. Henry Preston, the fellow who dreamed up the Frog Level Yacht Club, teaches a lesson on the economics of rolling your own cigarettes.

"I picked up the technique about five years ago in The Netherlands," he says. "The Dutch are famous for their cigars, of course. They used to own Indonesia and cultivated good-tasting tobacco. Cigarettes you roll yourself are a lot cheaper and the flavor's different from pre-rolled. I save about $2.35 a pack. For me, that adds up to about $1,000 a year."

T. E. Bowling tolerates talk of cigarettes with smoke-free lungs just as he cracks open dozens of beers a day and never brings a bottle to his lips. He overlooks even the wildest political diatribes and gigs with arm-folded stoicism.

The Frog Level Service Station is rarely mentioned in tourist guidebooks for the Commonwealth of Virginia, yet folks from all over the world have found it. First lured in by the unforgettable name, they're kept there awhile by the unassuming hospitality of a legendary bartender who, in his mid-eighties, generally comes in about 9 A.M. six days a week and stays until the last drink is downed. It's the only way he knows to make sure things run smoothly at the service station without gasoline and the yacht club without a yacht.

The Frog Level Service Station

Located near the Historic Crab Orchard Museum outside of Tazewell, Virginia. The original two-lane US routes 19 and 460 intersect with route 16 at Frog Level.

(276) 988-2085

Eating Arvil Burgers at Tootie's in Willie Boom

Arvil Vance and the hamburger that carries his name. *Photo by Larry Smith.*

It's often said that teaching isn't a one-way flow of information. Teachers not only impart knowledge, they absorb it from their students. It's common for teachers to say, "I've learned as much from my students as they have from me."

In fall 2005, I began teaching a course called "The Foodways of Appalachia" at East Tennessee State University. One of the requirements is an oral history. Students go out into the field with tape recorders and interview food people. Vickie Phillips was one of those students. For her project, she chose a place called Tootie's on the Tennessee side of Bristol and interviewed a man named Arvil Vance, son of the original owner.

The Arvil Burger in all its oniony opulence. *Photo by Larry Smith.*

For some reason, probably because it's on Highway 421—not my regular route into Bristol—Tootie's had escaped my hamburger/hot dog radar screen. As one of my readers in Oak Ridge says about establishments I've covered, Tootie's is "a Fred place."

I learned from Vickie's interview transcription that Tootie's is Bristol's oldest restaurant, having opened in fall 1945, a few months after Claude Arvil Vance returned home from World War II. The yellow 1991 Lincoln parked out front was used for advertising the restaurant's sixtieth anniversary in 2005.

In the official record books of the city of Bristol, you won't find Tootie's listed, at least under the T's. The legal name of the business is Vance's Confectionary, since, in the early days, single-count candy was sold there.

Vickie's parents, Ray and Catherine Phillips, were two of the original customers back in the 1940s, and Ray's still coming there every Monday night for his "Deacons' Meeting." Like the restaurant, Catherine's got a nickname that stuck, also: Toodle.

For that matter, so does the community: Willie Boom. Arvil explains that across the road, where Food City stands now, there was once a big lake.

"People brought in logs and floated them up to a lumberyard, owned by a Mr. Willie. 'Boom' referred to the floating timbers."

I asked Arvil about the geographic confines of Willie Boom. "It's about a 1-mile radius," he said.

In the middle of the twentieth century, Tootie's was the only restaurant between State Street in Bristol and Mountain City. Arvil's dad, Claude, rode the 9:00 A.M. bus to downtown Bristol, where he managed the housewares and toy departments at H. P. King Company. He whistled all the way. Claude whistled constantly. He whistled before he could talk, and that's the origin of the restaurant's name, Tootie's, spelled out in an arc of orange and yellow Styrofoam letters on the wall beside a signed photograph of former Baltimore Colts quarterback Johnny Unitas.

"Dad was jolly, happy all the time," recalls Arvil. "He loved the kids."

Arvil, an unassuming pipefitter who runs East Tennessee Vending and Amusement, is not the kind of person who'd name a hamburger after himself. The Arvil Burger was so named because of the insistence of a customer.

"One day, about twenty years ago, when I was working daylight to dark, I missed breakfast," remembers Arvil. "Then it got busy, and I hadn't had lunch. By 2 or 3 o'clock, it had slowed down, and I was very hungry, so I

Tootie's sports classic cab stand architecture. *Photo by Larry Smith.*

fixed me a big hamburger, threw some chopped onions in the center, added some garlic salt, and fried it.

"A customer walked in and asked me what it was. I told him, and he said, 'Fix me one.' I said, 'You can have this one.'"

The customer implored him to call it something other than a big hamburger and suggested Arvil lend his own name, which he did.

In May 2005, Arvil upped the size of his burger to 10 ounces. Eighteen to twenty folks at Bill Gatton's car place usually each order one for lunch.

"A hamburger won't kill you," insists Arvil. "Dad lived a long life and he ate one almost every day."

It's the massive size, the freshly ground meat, the onions cooked inside the patty, the sprinkling of garlic salt, the bright red tomatoes, even in February, and the uncooked disks of onion on top that make this hamburger so prized around Willie Boom.

Arvil points out that even his quarter pound burger is 4 1/2 ounces. For lesser appetites, the Tootie Burger is small and square.

The all-meat hot dog is cooked on a roller grill, and Tootie's offers a 100 percent beef kosher dog which can be deep-fried if customers request it, says longtime manager Helen Cook.

Tootie's has never served alcohol, but that hasn't stifled the liveliness of the political discourse there. Arvil says it's primarily a Democratic hangout, "but we've supported Republicans and Democrats both." He says his customers have a 90 percent success rate in predicting outcomes of elections.

Arvil and his wife Jane have a nice home of their own in Bristol, but Arvil remembers living in the restaurant building during his younger days.

"I took my baths right there where the counter is now, that was the living room, took my baths there in a washtub," he told Vickie. "No one would be able to open Tootie's and make it any more. Like your Mom and Dad, a lot of people had their first date or their first hot dog or hamburger here, listened to their first jukebox, or played their first pinball machine."

And they keep coming back. Their children keep coming back. Their grandchildren. All for goodness from the grill and stories about the lively little boy who whistled.

Tootie's
1310 Virginia Avenue
Bristol, Tennessee
(423) 764-6215